INTIMATE
EATING

Duke University Press   *Durham and London*   2022

INTIMATE
EATING

Racialized Spaces and Radical Futures   **Anita Mannur**

© 2022 Duke University Press
All rights reserved
Printed in the United States of America on acid-free paper ∞
Cover design by Matt Tauch
Typeset in Whitman and Helvetica by Copperline Book Services

Library of Congress Cataloging-in-Publication Data
Names: Mannur, Anita, author.
Title: Intimate eating: racialized spaces and radical futures /
Anita Mannur.
Description: Durham: Duke University Press, 2022. | Includes
bibliographical references and index.
Identifiers: LCCN 2021019896 (print) | LCCN 2021019897 (ebook)
ISBN 9781478015208 (hardcover)
ISBN 9781478017820 (paperback)
ISBN 9781478022442 (ebook)
Subjects: LCSH: Food habits—Cross-cultural studies. | Food—Social
aspects. | Food habits—Social aspects. | Asian Americans—Food. | South
Asians—Food. | Asian Americans—Social life and customs. | South
Asians—Social life and customs. | Cooking, Asian—Social aspects. |
BISAC: COOKING / Essays & Narratives | SOCIAL SCIENCE / Ethnic Studies /
American / Asian American Studies
Classification: LCC GT2850. M366 2022 (print) |
LCC GT2850 (ebook) | DDC 394.12—dc23
LC record available at https: //lccn.loc.gov/2021019896
LC ebook record available at https: //lccn.loc.gov/2021019897

Cover art: Sita Kuratomi Bhaumik, *To Curry Favor* (detail), 2015.
Site-specific installation. Shankill Castle, County Kilkenny, Ireland.
Turmeric, cumin, coriander, garam masala, and chili powder from
Kilkenny Halal Foods and Shortis Wong Deli applied to the walls of
the conservatory. Courtesy of the artist.

In memory of David Lenson (1945–2020)

Contents

Acknowledgments

I began thinking about this book many years ago, and only in the wake of one of the most trying periods of my life was I finally able to start seeing the ideas clustering in my head as a book. I started to write in earnest at a low point in my life, and I completed the revisions during the COVID-19 pandemic. To say that duress and trauma were the waters through which I swam in order to finish this book is an understatement.

This book is about intimate eating publics. It is about the unexpected intimacies that emerge among people who are not direct kin but nonetheless feel so deeply like family. It is about finding love and nourishment in strange places. It is about valuing the fleeting moments of intimacy that feel precious against the pressures of heteronormative time. It is about finding a way to hold dear those who care about one another, not because they have to, but because they want to. Those people are who buoyed me forward and to whom I am most grateful for sustaining me in every way possible. They helped me find a way to the shore when life felt unimaginably cruel.

This project quite simply would not exist without the patient support of my editor, Courtney Berger. I am indebted to her for her discerning eye and her belief in this book, long before I had even begun to imagine it was possible. Thank you for being the best editor a person could ask for. The work also would not have been possible without the incredible team at Duke University Press: Sandra Korn, William Page, and Susan Albury. Much gratitude to

Melanie Adley at Ideas on Fire for her careful work on the index. The manuscript is so much stronger because of the careful and assiduous readings from the three anonymous reviewers.

I am grateful to all of the artists and cultural producers who kindly allowed me to reproduce their work here: Miho Aikawa, Sita Kuratomi Bhaumik, Lawrence Dai, Abhijeet Kini, Michael Rakowitz, Jon Rubin, and Dawn Weleski. My gratitude also goes to New York University Press for allowing me to reproduce a portion of the chapter "Perfection on a Plate: Readings in the South Asian Transnational Queer Kitchen" that appeared in *Eating Asian America* (New York: New York University Press, 2013). Further thanks go to Taylor and Francis for granting permission to include a portion of my article "Eat, Dwell, Orient: Food Networks and Asian/American Cooking Communities" that appeared in the journal *Cultural Studies*, available at http://www.tandf online.com.

During the early months of the COVID-19 pandemic, I found refuge in writing groups led—not surprisingly—by fierce and brilliant women. Close to home, I am grateful to the Howe Writing Center at Miami University, particularly Ann Updike for organizing these virtual write-ins. This structural support for writing and research crucially helped me. I have much gratitude for Jacquie and Nadine Mattis, the brilliant minds behind Easton's Nook. A retreat there in summer 2019 gave me the start I needed, and the continued Saturday morning virtual write-ins allowed me to feel connected to a community of women of color and to remember that we often write because we have to. We write to save our lives. We write to imagine a better and more just world. And thanks to Jacquie and Nadine for recognizing the importance of mentoring and providing structure for writing, for the delicious meals and never-ending supply of the world's best banana bread, for reminding me when to walk away from my screen and take a walk—I will always be grateful.

I am thankful to my colleagues, all of whom make Miami a place I am happy to work. I thank cris cheek, Stefanie Dunning, Erin Edwards, Andrew Hebard, Elisabeth Hodges, Katie Johnson, Tim Lockridge, Tim Melley, TaraShea Nesbit, Liz Wardle, and my indefatigable chair, Madelyn Detloff.

As an interdisciplinary scholar, I've had the good fortune to travel among many brilliant people. Many of you were kind enough to invite me to speak at your institutions, and I am grateful for that tremendous labor and kindness. I am grateful to my hosts and the audiences at Christ University Bangalore, Manipal University, Northwestern University, Old Dominion University, Radboud University, Rice University, Rutgers University, Swarthmore College, University of Alaska–Anchorage, University of Amsterdam, University of Buffalo, University of California, Davis, University of California, San Diego, University of Cincinnati, University of Connecticut–Storrs, University of Illinois at Urbana-Champaign, University of Leipzig, University of Massachusetts, Amherst, University of Minnesota, University of Nevada, Las Vegas, University of Pennsylvania, and University of Texas at Austin. I thank the friends, students, and colleagues in real and virtual spaces who have supported my work in multiple ways: reading chapters, inviting me to present my work, freewheeling during conversations, or simply just being an ally. I thank Suzanne Aalberse, Anupama Arora, Aimee Bahng, Ben Balthaser, Nila Bhattacharjya, Tina Chen, Floyd Cheung, Paul Conway, Iyko Day, Jigna Desai, Tracey Deutsch, Rebecca Dingo, Abby Dubisar, Chris Eng, Tara Fickle, Cat Fung, Donna Gabaccia, Jose de la Garza-Valenzuela, Mike Gill, Jennifer Glaser, Bill Johnson Gonzalez, Jennifer Ho, Michelle Huang, Allan Punzalan Isaac, Doug Ishii, Matthew Frye Jacobson, Joseph Jeon, Simi Kang, Dinidu Karunanayake, Zeynep Kilic, Jina Kim, Jinah Kim, Kareem Khubchandani, Casey Kuhajda, Jim Lee, Josephine Lee, Wendy Lee, Danielle Lemmett, Sidne Lyon, Martin Manalansan, Bakirathi Mani, LuMing Mao, Jürgen Martschukat, Annemarie Mol, Linde Murugan, Asha Nadkarni, Lei Ouyang, Josephine Park, Joseph Ramirez, Sangeeta Ray, Zelideth Maria Rivas, Juana Maria Rodriguez, Sharmila Rudrappa, Ellen Samuels, Bryant Simon, Marlene Tromp, Monique Truong, Chris Vials, Jenny Wang, Laura Anh Williams, Psyche Williams-Forson, Nicolyn Woodcock, and Ji-Yeon Yuh. Tim August, Ajay Bailey, Robert Ji-Song Ku, and Mark Padoongpatt, my fellow travelers in Asian American/Asian diaspora food studies, have been steadfast colleagues and the best of interlocutors. My writing and thinking are so much the better for their astute feedback to and critical engagement with my work.

My Cincinnati friends who have been so important in my everyday life deserve all the love, and no words are adequate to thank them. Nonetheless I will try. Thank you to Jen Cohen, Mary Jean Corbett, Madelyn Detloff, Theresa Kulbaga, and Elaine Miller for being there during the good, the bad, and the SAD. Thank you all for making Cincinnati home. We have weathered much together, and I am fortunate to have this fierce group of women in my life.

I wish, most especially, to thank my dearest friends and family. Christine Mok is a friend and beloved colleague whose kindness and generosity are unparalleled, whose elegance and acuity I will always admire, and whose unflagging support is always welcome in my life even if I will never forgive her for abandoning me in Cincinnati. Jason Palmeri is an incomparable human being. He has picked me up more times than either of us probably wishes to recall, stood by me through every moment of this project, believed in me at every turn, and been the best friend, best traveler in the world of food, and best colleague a person could wish for. Gaile Pohlhaus has been a staunch ally and confidante. My ride-or-die for life, my conference wife of more than twenty years, Cathy Schlund-Vials is my person. In the two decades that we have been friends, we have grown together, and she has been there for me through everything. I also thank my mother, Shobana Mannur, for always believing in me. She is the best person I know, and I am truly lucky that someone as discerning as her believes the same of me as well. I am also grateful to my dad, H. G. Mannur, who remains firmly in my corner. I can't imagine life without any of these amazing human beings.

Interspecies love is real, and Keith and Owens Mannur are the loves of my life. Although they will always love tuna and catnip more than they love me, they are furballs of delight who have kept my spirits up in more ways than they will ever know. Any mistakes in this book can be attributed to their studied indifference to my intellectual pursuits.

I dedicate this book to my late mentor and professor, David Lenson. David passed away as I was putting the final touches to this book. He taught me many things about writing. David's life ended before I was ready to say goodbye, but his words and spirit live on in me and in the many other students whose lives he touched. For being the very first person who so many years ago encouraged a naïve twenty-five-year-old that she had something to say about food, I will always be grateful. I remember David with love and respect. Now and always.

In her artistic oeuvre, the multiracial visual artist Sita Kuratomi Bhaumik uses multimedia and tactile approaches to food and race in the United States to subvert what she describes as the "hegemony of vision."[1] We have developed a critical vocabulary within cultural studies and ethnic studies to think about visual culture, because often art that "deals with other senses suffers from under theorization."[2] Much of Bhaumik's artistic work revolves around the use of curry, that ubiquitous signifier of Indianness, even as curry itself is a British colonial invention. For Bhaumik, curry was a way "for colonizers to contain the vastness of empire and consume the difference within it," even though curries varied dramatically in taste, smell, and texture among the various places they were consumed.[3] Thus her use of *curry* is not coincidental. Bhaumik asks: "What is curry? One, a delicious food. Two, a wholly inadequate word to describe a wide diversity of dishes served around the world."[4] Imagining curry as malodorous and "out of place" in American homes and certainly within the space of the sanitized museum is part of what motivates her "curry art." Bhaumik's interest in this perceived incongruence led her in 2011 to create an installation titled "The Curry Institute" at the Sheehan Gallery at Whitman College.

Here Bhaumik designed a three-walled installation that included four pieces of art titled "Curry Cartography," "Sweet, Sour, Salty, Bitter, Curry," "Gilt," "Laced." These works, respectively, were a site-specific map of the world created with a combination of Behr paint and curry powder, a table filled with curry-scented jars, a site-specific curry-scented wallpaper, and a bottle of

Figure I.1 "To Curry Favor." Site-specific installation at the Begovich Gallery, California State University, Fullerton. Materials: curry powder from Oasis Food Market in Oakland, California, adhesive. 4 × 15 ft. © 2011. Photo credit: Sita Bhaumik.

curry-scented eau de toilette. The wallpaper invited people to engage 1
senses at once: while looking at the aesthetic design of the print, one
also lean in close to touch the walls of the art gallery—behavior typ
proscribed by art galleries and museums—and smell the artwork. The
invited people to pick them up, open the lids, and smell the aromas wafting
from what appeared to be colorless liquids. And the map of the world didn't
merely map the routes by which spices traveled from India and Asia to Europe;
rather, the interactive map allowed gallery visitors to place pins over the locations around the world where they had eaten dishes that could be described
as curry, however broadly construed. In this way, the journey of spices was
not being determined by their colonial and commoditized travels but by the
intimate ways in which museumgoers experienced "curry" in their lives and
through senses other than the visual. As Bhaumik notes, she wanted to find a
way for curry to travel, and to chronicle the malleable meanings that accrue
around the signifier of curry.[5]

At the heart of the exhibition was the issue of whether the odor of curry
would have a disruptive effect on the other installations, because the smell
refused to stay in place and migrated throughout the space of the museum. In
essence, the private was out of place because it entered into the public realm.
Bhaumik's exhibit suggests that such unruliness is an undesirable feature of
immigrant and racialized bodies. Museums, after all, are typically ordered
spaces where artwork remains in place and one is transported to a sanitized
space where unruliness is kept at bay. Similarly, immigrants and refugees and
people of color are reminded often of the unruliness of their bodies and of
their foods, and where and how abject or aberrant bodies need to be mindful
of the spaces they can occupy. But the refusal of Bhaumik's smell-oriented art
to stay in place suggests that food creates unexpected adjacencies and intimacies. Smell, after all, does not remain in place but wafts where it wishes.

Race, as Elam et al. have suggested, is not merely a problem of visuality
but one that stems from bodily inscriptions of otherness.[6] Bhaumik's curry
art falls within the spectrum of edible metaphors that combine vision, taste,
and smell. When an encounter with difference interrupts the experience of
sociality, what might be some of the ways in which food, typically imagined
as a source of comfort, can be reconfigured in order to productively mine the
value of the space of discomfort, conflict, and the thorny, as Bhaumik so art-
fully renders explicit in her olfactory installations? Bhaumik notes that her
desire to think about curry as art began when she read a post on a website in
which someone complained about the smell of curry emanating from a neigh-

bor's home. To her question asking what she should do, another person posted the xenophobic response, "Call the INS [Immigration and Naturalization Service] and have them deported."[7] In this context, the complainant was making visible their overt racism and a refusal to accept the intimate proximity of the indelibly foreign-seeming body, wholly unassimilable to the nation. And the knee-jerk response (whether serious or not) to call the authorities accessed a narrative that those who embody difference deserve to be expelled from the nation. To wit, what kinds of questions can one ask about the radical asymmetries emerging from a culture of intolerance that structure what is deemed edible and inedible, who belongs and who doesn't?

I begin with this discussion of Bhaumik's art to center the questions that animate this book: How might the culinary be mobilized to strategically critique, advance, and contravene into discourses of intimacy? How do ideas of public and private become central in thinking about the provenance of food? In particular, how can food be used—not to tell us what people eat per se, but to illuminate how radical publics and intimate spaces of belonging (and unbelonging) are created for nonnormative subjects? With an intellectual debt to Michael Warner's work on publics and counterpublics, *Intimate Eating* argues that it is nearly impossible to imagine a social world without the existence of publics. "Publics," Warner argues, are "queer creatures."[8] In our heavily mediated worlds, many activities are oriented to publics. Whether they appear in the form of television, movies, or other visual and print media, texts cannot make meaning without their publics. Warner proceeds to argue that the publics that consume these media are not necessarily populated only by those who directly belong to our worlds, but also by those who function as strangers. A public, therefore, is at once familiar, intimate, and strange. I build on Warner's logics to ask what happens when eating occurs within the realm of the public. Further, the particular dynamics with which this book engages take seriously the notion that eating does not operate under an optics of color blindness or cultural deodorization.[9] Seeing queer bodies and bodies of color eating together produces different *narratives* of intimacy while also inviting different *kinds* of scrutiny of the bodies that are eating and the foods being prepared.

To this end, no two publics are the same across time or space. Yet markedly different power dynamics are at work when one shifts focus from thinking about eating within the realm of the private (the home) to consider instead how eating occurs within the realm of the public (restaurants, office spaces, food trucks). Recognizing that certain forms of intimacy occur within the home via eating and cooking, this book examines how nonnormative intimacies can be brokered through food in the realm of the public. I look at how social worlds—the queer publics Michael Warner describes—are formed, mediated, and sustained through forms of eating with the recognition that different forms of sociality structure the experience of eating. Attending to the notion that eating publics contain ambiguities and contradictions, this book advances an understanding of the public that works with its possibilities but also recognizes its limitations. A public in and of itself is not radical. Rather, it is how one inhabits the space of the public, how one remakes the public, how one reshapes the public to accommodate difference beyond a vision of neoliberal multiculturalism that lends the intimate eating public its radical potential. The argument I put forth about the intimate eating public underscores that how one eats, consumes, and distributes food must reconfigure how we think about networks of intimacy beyond the familial, the heteronormative, the couple, and the nation.

What is an intimate eating public? I suggest that an intimate eating public is a vexed and contested space that is hybrid and evolving. Every act of eating with others, or alone, is a form of intimacy. And yet each gesture of eating is laced with multiple meanings that acquire differential public meanings. Eating is contingent on socioeconomic status, race, and gender. Whom we eat with, how we eat, and how these rituals are imagined are important, particularly in works that consciously rework how we think about the connection among eating, intimacy, and the public. *Intimate Eating* takes seriously the notion that whether eating occurs in a restaurant, at an office desk, after a cooking lesson, or after cooking with others, it establishes a form of kinship that refuses to be contained by narratives of heteronormativity. Therein lies the potential for radical intimacies to emerge.

Not all eating, however, focuses on public meanings. As Clare A. Sammells and Edmund Searles note, "the conspicuous consumption of public feasting seems an ancient and ubiquitous part of human sociality but this is distinct from the realm of quotidian eating in family homes, market stands, diners, and other less ostentatious spaces."[10] They also note that the term *semipublic* refers to the ambiguous, hybrid spaces that connect producers, merchants, and consumers to friend- or kin-based feasts, neighborhood restaurants, village markets, and roadside stands—places that are not quite private but not quite public either.[11] Following this lead, *Intimate Eating* focuses on narratives in which those who occupy the spaces where eating occurs intimately understand these spaces to cross the seemingly rigid demarcations that would separate the public from the private. It is to this end that I use the term *intimate eating publics*, remaining cognizant that a commitment to tear down the structures of neoliberal multiculturalism belies the formation of this kind of radical eating public.

Within food studies, several scholars have attended to the collapse of the distinction of private and public that is, as Sammells and Searles note, "created, maintained or understood in semi-public dining spaces."[12] Further, Karla Erickson argues that restaurants often strive to reproduce the intimate, personal ambience of eating at home and are productively thought of as "third spaces."[13] Within studies of food and sociality, third spaces are something other than either domestic spaces or workplaces but are nonetheless essential for community building and public sociality. As restaurants incorporate elements of both commercial activities and noncommercial domesticity, they are somewhere in between public and private. This book engages with eating cultures where the lines between the public and the private are contextual and in flux, even as the boundaries between the two remain important. To wit, I argue that the boundaries between the public and the private are not arbitrary or meaningless. Rather, the public and the private intersect to create new spaces that give rise to alternative cultural imaginings that, at their best, reimagine radical possibilities for nonnormative bodies.

Within postcolonial and diaspora studies, however, third spaces carry an entirely different meaning. As Homi Bhabha notes, the third space is a "hybrid" space that doesn't simply emerge from a combination of the other two. Rather, the third space "displaces the histories that constitute it and sets up new structures of authority and new cultural logics."[14] In this book, I ask how these intimate eating publics are critical third spaces—both in culinary and in diasporic terms—wherein food, forms of eating, and commensality become sites from which to resist imperialist policies, homophobia, practices of racial profiling, and articulations of white supremacy.

To mine most productively the tension between the meanings of the third space in both food studies and postcolonial and transnational studies, I turn to works with an explicit transnational bent that also engage specifically with the culinary practices and rhetorics of transnational South Asian and Arab contexts. My archive for this book includes the South Asian film *The Lunchbox*; several popular memoirs including Elizabeth Gilbert's *Eat, Pray, Love*, Julie Powell's *Julie & Julia*, and the lesser-known *Ginger and Ganesh* by Nani Power; the romance novel *Bodies in Motion* by Mary Anne Mohanraj; the cooking show *The Great British Bake Off*; and two culinary art–inspired ventures, including the now-defunct Conflict Kitchen and art installations by Michael Rakowitz titled *The Spoils of War* and *Enemy Kitchen*. I argue that this particular constellation of texts and cultural objects—spanning different locales across the United States (after September 11, 2001), the United Kingdom (after Brexit), and India—allows us to inquire into how racialized South Asian and Arab brown bodies become visible through acts of culinary intimacy at moments of heightened anxiety about brown and queer bodies. In assembling this particular archive, I look to works that do not neatly map onto areas of study that have often been privileged within the academy. Rather, I bring works together, in some ways following what Gayatri Gopinath dubs "queer curation." For Gopinath, a scholar of queer South Asian diasporas whose work has always inspired the way I think about cultural critique, acts of queer curation are fundamentally about caring for the objects one writes about while also attending to the ways that cultural analysis can go beyond revealing "coevalness or sameness." As Gopinath so wonderfully puts it, queer curation is about the "co-implication and radical relationality of seemingly disparate racial formations, geographies and temporalities."[15] Assembling, finding, and documenting cultural texts—some that enjoy mainstream appeal and others that may be of only a fleeting interest to some—is part of a queer curatorial project. It is a way to reaffirm that cultural texts produced by QTBIPOC artists and writers are important regardless of the size of their audiences. In the data-driven neoliberal academy, we are always asked to document the value of certain fields of study. Numbers drive the game, and the small gets jettisoned. Queer curation is embedded instead in practices of care and aims to find connections among texts and cultural pasts that might seem discontinuous. To Gopinath's assessment I would add that this kind of methodological practice also takes seriously the study and exploration of texts that are deemed frivolous, unimportant, subliterary, or all three. Many of the objects I have assembled for this study are not important because of some perceived long-standing cultural value. In all likelihood, they will fade into obscurity within a decade. And yet they remain important because they allow us to reorient how we think about certain cultural processes while making legible the ways in which eating can be about possibilities and potentials other than securing the good life of heteronormative bliss.

In my own act of queer curation, then, I stage a conversation among this series of texts across varied locations to focus on the idea of how the act of eating within the realm of the public allows us to see where and how that act becomes freighted with meanings that go beyond normative understandings of commensality. Discussion about South Asian and Arab transnational food-ways are my focus because cuisines associated with South Asian and Arab sub-jectivities are often policed vigilantly and imagined to be out of place within the realm of the public. Although we might typically link these spaces through moments of war and neoliberal disaffection, my readings across the chapters suggest that we can also link them through the ways in which certain food-ways allow us to think through the tension between "anxiety" and comfort (food). Because of its provenance among "enemy" nations, Arab cuisine is in-credibly fraught in the United States. Restaurants that serve Iraqi food, for example, must often use more benign monikers such as "Middle Eastern." Similarly, South Asian food—often understood through its extremities of be-ing too hot, too oily, too spicy, too pungent—also constantly has to negotiate the terms under which it is presented and consumed among its publics. Thus, each chapter examines how cultural texts strategically center the act of eating in the service of imagining different kinds of publics—ones that continually reimagine forms of belonging for marginalized bodies.

Across this book, I suggest that it is nearly impossible to imagine a social world without the existence of publics. And yet these publics are not neces-sarily populated only by those who directly belong to our worlds; they also include those who might more typically be considered strangers.[16] In turn-ing my attention to the idea of the eating public, in this book I ask how social worlds are formed, mediated, and sustained through forms of eating, recog-nizing that different forms of sociality can structure the experience of eating. In attending to the world-building function of intimacy that Lauren Berlant describes, I look to the kinds of intimacies that "bypass the couple."[17] Berlant implicitly argues that what we can think of as minor intimacies develop alter-nate aesthetics and ways of being. Intimacy, as I understand it, is not about imagining lives teleologically oriented toward securing forms of normativity or couplehood that are buoyed by the desires of the nation. The desire for a normative kind of intimacy so easily eliminates from analysis those for whom access to this purported "good life"—intimacy with its continual attachment to heteronormative happiness—is not simply just unattainable but also often undesirable. I think here most specifically in the terms Berlant usefully pro-vides. They note that this almost overbearingly hegemonic version of a kind of intimacy oriented toward a telos of heteronormative happiness is a kind of narrative or story. And yet, as they note, "those who don't or can't find their way in that story—the queers, the single, the something else—can become so easily unimaginable, even often to themselves."[18] To imagine how it is that the queers, the singles, and the "something elses" find ways to create imaginable narratives is an important critical trajectory of this book.

As someone who separated from my spouse in my mid-forties, I find myself particularly compelled to hold space for these queer and queer-adjacent subjects who are often imagined as lamentable figures in need of rescue or pity. If these nonnormative subjects are so easily removed from these kinds of narratives to the extent that they can no longer even imagine ways forward, part of the task of Asian American literary and cultural critique is not merely to install these subjects as viable but to read narratives, broadly conceived, as ones that reorient us toward other forms of intimacy wherein the goal is not necessarily unmitigated happiness or securing the "good life" but—at the risk of sounding Pollyannaish—ways of being in the world that are radically fulfilling in other ways.

To this end, I take a page from the work of Asian American literary scholar Nicolyn Woodcock. In her article on forms of intimacy in Asian American literature, Woodcock poses the question of what worlds can be built when narratives of intimacy are placed at the center of reading Asian American literature and culture. Woodcock asserts that although "common sense suggests that personal relationships form as a result of choice, consent and affection—and that they are not the business of the state—thinking of the intimate contacts between Asian and American through such traditional notions conceals the forced nature of US imperial relations with the Asia-Pacific regions."[19] Although Woodcock's archive comprises works that directly engage forms of militarization, the heuristic she develops is useful insofar as it illuminates how the state and official apparatuses contravene into the most seemingly innocuous and nonpoliticized relationships in ways that enable or militate against certain kinds of intimacy.

Food studies, a wide-ranging interdisciplinary area of research that has received thorough scholarly attention, has become an established area of intellectual inquiry. Since I published *Culinary Fictions* in 2010, critical work in food studies has exploded, and academic and nonacademic presses continue to publish a range of titles in this area. Despite the growth of critical work in the field over the past two decades, a need remains for more politicized readings of food in the humanities that press on the radical possibilities for imagining commensality. Scores of volumes tell us what people eat and why they eat what they eat. But a critical lacuna (filled by only a handful of texts) exists that strategically centers the culinary, not to ask what people eat, but to treat the culinary as a starting point from which to inquire into how different forms of embodiment—racial, sexual, and gendered—use food to dismantle the often stifling notion that we can overcome difference by eating together as a means of seeing the basic humanity of people whom we deem suspicious.[20] At heart, my particular intellectual intervention into food studies is to drive home the point that the culinary can serve as a heuristic to articulate nonnormative forms of intimacy that go beyond the idea of queerness as consonant with sexuality alone. To this end, my work owes an intellectual debt to the methodological orientations of queer of color critique. In particular, I work to unearth the multivalent gestures of pleasure and social justice that can underpin the modalities of eating.

The texts I work with all respond to contemporary social justice movements that highlight how late capitalist formations and neoliberalism have created spaces that are unrelentingly hostile to nonnormative bodies—queer, immigrant, female—that seem to be out of place and out of time. These texts use the discursive and affective value of food to enact their political and cultural work of imagining other worlds and possibilities. Although food is traditionally mobilized as a metaphor for the coming together of communities and the melding of differences, I argued against this logic in my previous work and sought instead to look at how food stigmatizes, isolates, and marginalizes communities of color, immigrants, single people, and queer people. The logic that eating together brings people together has always puzzled me, and I had only begun to think this through when I wrote *Culinary Fictions*. *Intimate Eating* presses this logic further by theorizing what we can think of as neoliberal multiculturalism. Taking a cue from my previous work on palatability, I argue that we must understand neoliberalism as a force that structures multiculturalism in ways that celebrate normative forms of difference. Neoliberal multiculturalism names the kinds of difference that insist on a vision of familiality and familiarity securely bound up with normative understandings of personhood, family, and nation. Those who are queer, single, and otherwise nonnormative fall outside of this vision of multiculturalism precisely because they are too messy and complicated. A main trajectory in this book is to center those cultural objects and narratives that would strategically upend narratives of normative normalcy as the necessary end goal of eating together. The intimate eating public, I argue, is one necessarily at odds with this vision of neoliberal multiculturalism, and it responds to and reframes its underlying investments that often feel oppressive to those who do not fit so easily within a vision of a carefully curated multicultural, neoliberal nation.

At the same time that neoliberal multiculturalism orients itself toward a vision of coexistence that would see all differences as equal and desirable, it successfully reproduces its ideological investments by overtly valorizing forms of eating that take place within the private home. The home, after all, is a central apparatus for imagining and securing the "good life." And the dinner table in particular is that vital site where normative families reproduce themselves. *Except when they don't.* I have never understood why so much emphasis is placed on families eating together because, to be brutally honest, I hated family dinners. If anything, the latent hostility around my family dining table was a daily reminder of the artifice necessary to maintain the illusion that heteronormative familial arrangements were in any way, shape, or form beneficial to women and nonnormative subjects. For me, the dining table and mealtimes were always incredibly fraught. I grew up in a very traditional nuclear family, and my mother labored tirelessly every day to ensure my brother, father, and I had warm meals and fresh food.

As I grew up as a part of the South Asian diaspora in Malaysia, Australia, and Papua New Guinea, eating was as much about keeping the family together as it was about retaining and affirming cultural knowledge of Indianness. Everything was meticulously chopped and prepared by hand. Despite it being the 1980s, my mother never used shortcuts in her kitchen. Cooking was a labor of love for my mother, but it was also a respite from my father's unpredictable and toxic behavior. In the kitchen, she maintained autonomy. And still, despite knowing her food might be criticized, she labored to produce elaborate dishes for every meal. Canned foods were never part of our diet, nor were ready-made meals. My mother was raising two children in the diaspora, and she wanted us to grow up knowing Indian food. But mealtimes were always tense, in large part because of my father. For all intents and purposes he was an unyielding and exacting patriarch. At the dinner table, this took the form of his incredibly judgmental attitudes about the food my mother cooked. If she accidentally added too much chili powder, or perhaps not enough salt to the sambar or dal, he would fling the dish across the table and deem it inedible. If the *chapattis* weren't fresh, he would complain. If my mother prepared carrots, coconut, beets—any ingredients he did not like—he would yell at her because she seemingly did not care about his tastes. If she made eggplant for a second day in a row (never mind that he refused to drive her to the grocery store to buy other vegetables), we would all hear about it.

To this day, I hate eggplant with a fierceness that can only be understood with this history in mind. The caprice with which my father would judge meals as good, bad, or inedible made for incredibly tense meals. I would never know what might set him off, and although most meals passed with relative calm, a cloud always loomed overhead, threatening to drench us in an outpouring of my father's anger du jour. As a child I would eat as quickly as possible—sometimes not eating as much as I wanted to—and then escape to the kitchen to do the dishes before retreating to my room to do homework. In this way, I could avoid being accused of being lazy; after all, I was helping my mother do the housework. At the same time, doing the dishes allowed me to orient my body away from my father. The sound of running water would drown out the sound of his voice. I always heard my mother's voice gently cajoling me: "Just be nice." "Don't talk back, it'll be easier for you." "I'll bring you some *anna mosuru* [rice with plain yogurt] to your room later if you're still hungry." "Do it for me." I can barely write these words without tearing up at the thought of how much work my mother put into cooking, knowing it was thankless labor and would often result in painful admonishment. There is no recipe that allows one to produce the kind of meal that will always satisfy the capricious and yet predictably toxic desires of heteronormative cis male patriarchy.

To say I hated family mealtimes is an understatement, and yet for some reason, we always sat down together as a family for every meal throughout the entirety of my childhood. I can only understand this as the external manifestation of an ideological orientation that both my parents had so successfully internalized. Domesticity called for, even demanded, families eating together. Indeed, the seams of heteronormative normalcy and intimacy were stitched together by what sometimes felt like a laughably lamentable attempt to adhere to the notion that the family that eats together stays together.

And yet, the dining table was also the site of other anxieties. It was where my father would hold court and verbally lambast my brother, my mother, and me for our perceived failings and indiscretions. To this day, unless I am hosting a dinner party, I find it incredibly difficult to sit at a dining table for an everyday meal. The silence at the dining table I now have, as a single woman—that I so craved as a child—is deafening because it feels like too little, too late. Eventually, a time came when my nuclear family ceased speaking to one another. My brother hasn't spoken to or seen my parents since 1994. I tolerate my father but I hold my mother very dear to my heart. I am the only person in my family who speaks to all three other members of the family, and I weary of it. Eating together certainly did not do its ideological work of saving this family.

At the age of eighteen, I left Port Moresby, Papua New Guinea, and went to college as far away as I could—two hemispheres away, in Madison, Wisconsin. There I had a temporary respite from these forms of eating. I learned to enjoy meals and not be constantly on edge—something I kept with me through my graduate school days in Amherst, Massachusetts. Sadly, that feeling also eventually disappeared a few years into my marriage when my then-husband decided to become vegetarian and refused to eat anything I cooked. The injury to me felt particularly acute because we had fallen in love over meals and I had painstakingly learned to make the foods that my white Midwestern husband loved: meatloaf, lasagna, macaroni and cheese, mashed potatoes. Once again, mealtimes felt fraught. I love meat with a zeal that might be unbecoming of a lapsed Brahmin. I would cook for myself and he would eat frozen foods because I had zero interest in preparing two meals, especially if one involved piercing holes in plastic film and heating it in a microwave. I had not developed a robust and enviable set of culinary skills only to have them jettisoned in favor of Michelina's finest cheesy ziti. Going out for meals also became less interesting because he would insist on not sharing food. His meal was his and my hand would be playfully swatted away if I reached for a bite from his plate. We would only order as much food as we could eat and never try new dishes.

Eventually I tired of this nonsense, and around the same time I became friends with a queer man who shared my passion for food. During our commutes home from Oxford, Ohio, where we both worked, we would take circuitous paths back to the apartment building where we lived in Cincinnati to find the hidden culinary gems of our city, often located in the suburbs and occasionally across the river in nearby Kentucky. Meals became fun again. My friend and I would order more food than we could possibly consume. We would try all manner of immigrant food available in our city: Uzbek, Korean, Nepalese, Somali, Pakistani, Szechuan. Aware that it might appear unseemly to have too much fun with a man other than the one I was married to, I would try to include my husband on some of these culinary adventures. Despite repeat invitations, however, my husband would refuse to join us, saying that he would be left out of the conversation because my friend and I would inevitably not only want to talk about what we loved about this particular meal, but proceed to plan future meals. "All you and your fussband do is talk about food. I have nothing to say," my straight husband would complain. *Fussband* was his slightly derogatory and homophobic moniker for my friend: a portmanteau of "food husband" and a nod to the episode of *The Simpsons* called "The Food Wife." It wasn't long before I ceased inviting him to meals out with my friend. And it wasn't long thereafter that we ceased to be, period.

But of course we would have to eat with friends on other occasions. I have been fortunate to have friends who will meticulously plan meals and culinary itineraries if they know I am along for the ride. Often the excuse would be that I was a minor expert on food studies and so they needed to meet my expectations and standards. What can I say? Writing about food has its perks. I rarely have a bad meal when out with friends; it more often occurs when strangers invite me to a meal. On the rare occasion when my husband ate with us, my friends would sigh when I mentioned he was joining us. "Does he have to?" they would ask. "He's so fussy and seems to hate food. Why are you married to him anyway?" Perhaps they knew something about my failing marriage that I did not.

Unsurprisingly perhaps, we eventually divorced. I had noted how our meals had gradually become unpleasant over time. Although I can now describe the events with a clarity unavailable to me at the time, I barely noticed then how meals with my husband had progressively become as affectively fraught as the ones with my family. There was never the threat of physical abuse, but meals did not bring us together. Indeed, nothing about eating together helped to buttress our heteronormative familial arrangement. Rather, over time, eating with my friends and my queer *familia* became what sustained me. At home, food did not bring me closer to the ones I was supposed to love—my father, my brother, my husband. I experienced love, warmth, and friendship only when I sat down to meals with my chosen family of QTBIPOC. Occasionally I cooked for friends, but more often than not, feelings of joy came from shared meals in intimate public spaces with people whom I chose as family.

I share this rather long and noncontinuous history of my own fraught experiences with domesticity and shared meals as a way to drive home a minor but significant point. In my experience, meals rarely worked to maintain the smooth workings of heteronormativity. Familial intimacy required much more than shared meals. It required acts of caring and the kind of emotional labor that often goes unremarked when thinking about food. And at the same time that I was all too aware of how fraught eating in the domestic space could be, I found reprieve during meals eaten with friends in public spaces, most notably restaurants and occasionally in the semipublic spaces of our offices.

In the years after my divorce I was also able to find immense pleasure in solo dining. For a woman to eat alone is to invite pity, fear, or even reproach. But my own experiences with eating alone led me to find intimacy—good and bad—in unexpected places. I've often been told I have a kind face (despite my attempts to cultivate resting bitch face and my incredibly dexterous skills when it comes to throwing shade) and perhaps that is why strangers often come up to me when I am eating alone, inquire about what I am eating (I often order unusual things), and offer unsolicited opinions about their admiration of me for eating alone, my choice of meal, or the mere fact that I seem to actually enjoy eating. Waiters—usually men—are often delighted that I want a table of my own and that I want to linger over my meal. They frequently offer me small tasting portions (sometimes framed as being compliments of the chef) or tell me about the meal because I am clearly there for the food. On one occasion, at a restaurant with three Michelin stars, one of the waiters was so impressed that I lingered for three hours over a very expensive meal that he presented me with a copy of the leather-bound menu from the fabled restaurant. I had asked for a copy of the tasting menu, which he could not find. He returned with the menu, pressed it toward me, placed a finger to his lips, and said, "Shhh. Tell no one about this. It's my gift to you for so obviously enjoying your meal." In this way, strangers become intimate—albeit briefly—for the duration of my meal.

The pleasure of the solo meal is hard to explain. It is not always about securing happiness; it can be about a different kind of affective fulfillment. With apologies to Virginia Woolf, rather than a room of my own in which to write, what I really wanted was a table of my own.

Thus, building on my previous work, I posit that in this archive I have assembled, the culinary is central to an effort to imagine more just and democratic forms of political belonging that enhance our understanding of the work intimacy can do. Exploring these visions and the constructed worlds that enact these imaginings is central to this book. Buoyed by work in queer studies, critical ethnic studies, and studies of intimacy, this book problematizes how reformulated nationalisms and transnational subjectivities presented in even the most progressive of texts can often implicitly reproduce the idea that eating together can form new and more democratic publics. To this end, I implicitly suggest that even progressive texts that represent eating together can reproduce neoliberal ideologies.

Intimate Eating gestures to the possibility of understanding citizenship and human coexistence in new ways. In so doing it provides an account of how and why QTBIPOC subjects look radically different when we more stringently take stock of the ways in which how, where, and what we eat, smell, and see are related to how we shape, and are constructed by, our racial and ethnic worlds. At the same time, this book also urges us to consider how eating can be a form of sociality that operates at many levels—with the self (solitary), among strangers, and across generations. The book is an effort to press the implications of how cultural narratives strategically deploy food to posit the formation of alternative spaces of intimacy and belonging that traverse the private and the public to challenge this normative understanding of food that is always already about ushering in comfort and national belonging.

The first two chapters are closely related; they take up questions about the individual diner or stranger who strategically deploys the culinary to transform notions about intimacy and eating publics. I begin with the figure of the individual because we so often imagine dining and sociality to be about conviviality that is often exclusively about forms of kinship structured around normative structures like the couple or the family. And yet, what are the ways that a public can emerge around a solitary figure? To begin with the figure of the single is to center on the figure of the queer eater and to dislodge the notion that to eat alone is to embody the abject or to be misanthropic or a failed subject. Foregrounding forms of solitary eating is this book's way of asking us to decenter normative couplings that so often structure how eating is imagined. Even as the realities of many lives do not abide by these strictures of normativity, it is worth considering how pervasively the hegemonic ideal of commensality maps onto the cultural imagination. Together, these chapters examine how public spaces of cooking, and performances of cooking, become venues to articulate new kinds of intimacies that subtly work against a mandated form of heteronormative coupling. I argue that each text creates a space from which to imagine cooking and eating to be queer acts about satisfying one's needs as a single person or one's desires that exceed the strictures of marriage or coupling.

In chapter 1, I provide a close reading of the independent film *The Lunchbox*. As context, each day in the crowded city of Mumbai, five thousand men in white outfits (dubbed *dabbawallas*) rely exclusively on public transportation to transport 175,000 lunches across the massive city. The exclusively male workforce retrieves the iconic tiffin boxes from domestic spaces across the city and delivers them to office buildings in Mumbai, transporting meals each day from mothers, wives, and daughters to husbands, fathers, and sons. This system of dabbawallas—in place since the days of British colonialism—is a hallmark of this thriving cityscape and continues to serve as an iconic example of a successful form of business that is largely driven by labor-intensive work and navigation of public space. I begin with this chapter because the dabbawalla is an essential figure who allows the private to enter the public. He is a broker of a kind of intimacy that can occur within the public space. And yet, despite being the person who is constantly in proximity to the food itself, the nature of his position as alienated labor prevents him from establishing any kind of intimate kinship with the families he serves.

Chapter 1 focuses less on the travels and travails of the figure of the dabbawalla, and more on the narrative of intimacy that emerges within the film. An epistolary film, *The Lunchbox* explores what it means for the lunchbox to traverse the space of the city, from stranger to stranger, through an error in a seemingly perfect system. Using public transportation, the dabbawallas deliver home-cooked meals to offices with remarkable accuracy. *The Lunchbox* is about a potentially grievous error in a system where errors are few and far between. What if the wrong dabba goes to the wrong workplace? In the film, Ila's dabba accidentally ends up at the desk of Saajan Fernandes, a stranger. The pattern continues and each day Saajan returns the lunchbox with a note, and thus develops an epistolary romance of sorts. In closely examining this film, I explore the intimacy that develops across public and private spaces among strangers who never meet but form an intimate public simply through the act of sharing meals and letters.

Developing the idea that intimate eating publics often explode the binary between the public and the private, chapter 2 hones in on narratives of eating alone. The chapter juxtaposes two distinct kinds of cultural work. The first is a series of photos of people dining alone. In the series of photos taken by New York–based photographer Miho Aikawa, one notices the various ways in which individuals are photographed eating alone. Aikawa's photos are fascinating because of the ways in which they train us to reorient our gaze on the solo diner. What if, instead of seeing isolation and a lack of happiness, we saw scenes of solo eating as profound acts of intimacy brokered by a radically different relationship between the diner and their meal? The other work to which I turn in this chapter is *Bodies in Motion*, a diasporic romance novel by the Sri Lankan American writer, Mary Anne Mohanraj.

Although the novel narrates the story of a multigenerational Sri Lankan family in diaspora, it also includes the perspective of a female character who does not migrate. The single woman, deemed unworthy of marriage because she is not attractive enough and does not possess the cultural capital to make her worthy of entering into the marriage contract, is the one left behind—the single woman who is seemingly incapable of being loved—in stark contrast to the large family whose members all attain mobility and move to various nodes of the Sri Lankan diaspora. Drawing on the work of Jack Halberstam and Michael Cobb, I read the figure of the single woman who cooks for herself as a queer agent, not as a failed subject.

Centering on the scenes of cooking in the novel, my analysis asks what it means to stay in place and to want to earn the right to not migrate; or, to use Alicia Schmidt Camacho's terms, what might "el derecho de no migrar" look like for a woman whose desires cannot be accounted for via a teleological narrative of heteronormative migration?[21] I argue that the single nonmigrant female in this novel is a kind of queer failure in the terms Jack Halberstam might use to advance a critique of the typical teleological narrative of migration. As someone who eats alone but also is aware of how people watch her eat, the character Mangai creates an intimate eating public by deliberately creating a hybrid space wherein the private becomes public.

The last three chapters turn to the field of visual culture, public art, cooking shows, and digital space. I examine art installations that prompt engagements with the viscerality of race, empire, and globalization, and the use of digital media to construct intimate eating publics. Whereas chapters 1 and 2 focus on the idea of how intimate eating publics coalesce around the figure of the solitary eater, chapters 3, 4, and 5 turn to different modalities of alienation and commensality. The third chapter describes work where seemingly alienated individuals in large cities turn to online communities (the blogosphere and Craigslist) to create forms of intimacy with strangers. To a large extent, the chapter focuses on exploring the *rhetorical strategies* that bring strangers into close quarters. The fourth chapter extends this logic to some extent by looking to the *cultural logics* that very strategically bring strangers together to share meals in public spaces. Chapter 5 turns to a much beloved cooking show where strangers cook together. In sum, these chapters advance a critical reading practice that helps us to see that shared acts of eating can help us to identify the distinction among cultural differences and cultural diversity.

Chapter 3 moves away from writing *by* Asian Americans to look at work *about* Asian Americans. As its starting point, it examines Elizabeth Gilbert's best-selling *Eat, Pray, Love* (2007), a memoir that immediately captured the fancy of middle-class white women everywhere. Chronicling the travails of one year of her life, *Eat, Pray, Love* was among the first of a new wave of neoliberal feminist writings that centered on the growth of a white female feminist—seeking refuge in otherness—over the course of a year. Not unlike *Eat, Pray, Love* are two other memoirs, Julie Powell's *Julie & Julia* and Nani Power's *Gin-*

ger and Ganesh. This chapter examines this pair of culinary texts, similarly organized, that turn to digital media to build a narrative about a year-long experiment with food. Through this juxtaposition of two very similar texts, the chapter sets in motion a debate about how Asian Americanist critique can further our understanding of this subgenre of internet-based writing. Whereas most of the texts examined in this book actively refute neoliberal multiculturalism as a means of building an intimate eating public, the books explored in this chapter most explicitly *rely* on the tenets of neoliberal multiculturalism. Although my analysis remains critical of the latent implications of each text, I am not denigrating the value of either one nor dismissing their potential to articulate female subjectivity through the lens of the culinary. Rather, my interest in these particular texts derives from wanting to make sense of how writings by avowed feminists who make use of the internet to construct a form of gendered solidarity that ostensibly crosses lines of age, race, and class might also produce familiar neoliberal Orientalist orthodoxies that continue to marginalize communities of color, particularly women of color, in ways that mark a deep anxiety about the position of the middle-class white feminist in the contemporary racial moment. I examine how these texts use food to apparently build intimacy within the hybrid spaces of home/blog/memoir while at the same time producing narratives of white privilege.

Developing the thread of how intimacy is created in public spaces, chapter 4 turns to a very different example. In this chapter, I explore how the figure of the "enemy" is constructed in public culinary sites. The spaces I examine are Michael Rakowitz's performance art installation *Enemy Kitchen*, and Conflict Kitchen, a now-defunct takeout restaurant in Pittsburgh, Pennsylvania. Briefly, both of these are art installations devoted to the dissemination of culinary knowledge about nations and spaces the post-9/11 US nation-state has deemed enemy territories. Michael Rakowitz's *Enemy Kitchen* is a public art project that explores the relation between hospitality and hostility. Rakowitz and his mother collected and compiled recipes from the Baghdad area. They turned these recipes into dishes that US veterans of the Iraq War served from a food truck designed by the artist. Conflict Kitchen was a restaurant that served cuisine from countries with which the United States is in conflict. Each Conflict Kitchen iteration was augmented by events, performances, publications, and discussions that sought to expand the public's engagement with the culture, politics, and issues at stake within the region of focus. The restaurant rotated identities in relation to current geopolitical events.

In juxtaposing these sites and exploring the performative politics deployed within each context, I ask what it means to turn to the tactile, olfactory, and palatal in order to reflect on questions of US diplomacy and foreign policy that have advanced cultural xenophobia in the wake of the war on terror and 9/11. By focusing on the use of what I describe as "radical hospitality," I ask how meals in Rakowitz's art installations and the curated meals and menus of Conflict Kitchen become spaces to provide a counternarrative to xenophobia and the discourse of the enemy combatant. The very idea of hospitality is suggestive of the need for a public. As Michael Hernandez notes, "in the process of going out to eat, we enter a social world, taking part in a play of sociability within the confines of the marketplace."[22] This play of sociability, I suggest, is a hallmark of radical hospitality, wherein the diner necessarily enters into this sociable world and is invited to reflect on the profound inequities that structure eating worlds. To be welcomed into spaces like Conflict Kitchen or *Enemy Kitchen* is also to be invited to recognize that a different modality of sociability needs to be enacted for subjects who are often refused hospitality. Creating public spaces that welcome the presence of subjects and cuisines that have been treated with hostility, I argue, is central to the form of radical hospitality that animates these spaces. Creating a different kind of public that allows for productive intimacies to take place through the consumption and preparation of "enemy" food is one way to think about how the intimate eating public allows for the thoughtful and critical consumption of food.

The final chapter follows on the heels of the previous one by turning to the immensely popular television baking show *The Great British Bake Off.* Where Conflict Kitchen and *Enemy Kitchen* are provisional spaces or third spaces that center on the formation of an intimate public, the forms of intimacy in *The Great British Bake Off* emerge within the provisional space of the white baking tent, where a group of ten to twelve home cooks from across Britain gather week after week to bake all manner of sweets and savories. Not home, not office, and not restaurant, this space is yet another in which networks of affiliation, though provisional, serve to construct an image of a nation that establishes and renews its links in the intimate public sphere. The nation becomes an intimate space wherein baking together forms the basis of a shared vision of the future. Although the actors themselves are important to this vision of a nation in which centrifugal forces bring people together, the baking ingredients also establish the ethos of this nation's imaginary. I argue that in its construction of a multicultural, postcolonial utopia away from the realities of an exclusionary post-Brexit United Kingdom, race plays an important part in defining what can be baked into quintessentially British fare. Examining the role of the three South Asians who have appeared on the show (notably the season 6 winner, Nadiya Hussain), I explore how race and sensory difference play an important role in creating a sense of comfort on the popular baking show. I show how South Asian spices have a special place in every season of *The Great British Bake Off*; bakers have attempted to fuse curries, masalas, and chutneys with traditional fare. For the most part, the judges convey excitement at the prospect of a successful dish that would represent the ethnic flavors and spices of Britain's former colonies. I argue, however, that the domestication of Indian ingredients in UK kitchens and pantries also requires that we consider which aspects are rendered assimilable in order to enhance the flavor of British baked goods against the kinds of pungent spices that are seen as being too excessively foreign.

Collectively, these chapters signal a way forward in navigating the contours of imagining intimate eating publics that are undergirded by a logic of challenging the status quo. These spaces of eating are not simply about imagining food as that which brings people together; to the contrary, the sum total of stories and narratives that emerge from these chapters allows us to imagine alternate, queer, and often radical ways that marginalized communities can find spaces of belonging amid a world that is structured to obscure and often deny their existence.

If the dabba had the wrong markings and went to the incorrect recipient, was the dabbawalla wrong?
—Salman Rushdie, *The Satanic Verses*

In his review of Ritesh Batra's *The Lunchbox, New York Times* film reviewer Gardiner Harris summarizes the film thus:

> *The Lunchbox* is about the amazing dabbawallahs, who transport hot meals by Mumbai housewives to their deskbound husbands.[1] A rare mix-up leads to a connection between a woman trying to woo her husband through his stomach and a testy insurance claims adjuster sliding toward early retirement. The two pass notes in the lunchbox.[2]

A film that mobilizes the form of the epistolary to develop an intimacy among two strangers who would never have been likely to cross paths, *The Lunchbox* is one of the first feature films to prominently feature in its narrative trajectory the fabled Mumbai system of dabbawallas. The film's plot rotates around this system, which has been a mainstay in Mumbai's public culture for several decades. Every day a large workforce comprising more than five thousand men picks up home-cooked lunches from the kitchens of housewives in Mumbai. Relying exclusively on forms of public transportation, or on foot, or by bicycle, the dabbawallas then transport the tiffins or *dabbas* to the mens' workplaces. So efficient is the system that mistakes are purportedly one in a million. The story of *The Lunchbox* is about this minor, but potentially grievous, error. What if the wrong tiffin goes to the wrong workplace? In the film, Ila, an unhappy housewife, prepares elaborate lunches each day for her husband, whose interest in his wife and her cooking has long since waned. Quite by mistake, the dabba that Ila prepares for her husband ends up on the desk of an accountant, Saajan Fernandes. Saajan, in turn, is delighted to find a delicious home-cooked meal of *roti* and masala green beans replacing his standard restaurant dabba of *alu gobi*. When the pattern repeats the next day, Saajan returns the tiffin with a note to Ila, and thus develops an epistolary romance of sorts. The error in the delivery system continues, allowing an intimacy to grow among the two characters, who are each accustomed to the rhythms that come from the solitude of eating alone. Each day brings an ever more delicious meal from Ila, and each meal elicits another epistolary exchange between the two characters, furthering the bonds of intimacy among two strangers in one of the most densely populated cities in the world via one of its most hallowed and celebrated traditions—the dabbawalla system of food delivery.

Certainly, part of any major city's claim to modernity is the presence of a varied and diverse food scene. Mumbai, a complex and diverse metropolis, has long been characterized as a city with a robust food culture. Perhaps because of its high population density, restaurants, street food vendors, and other forms of public eating have thrived. And yet, for decades, a segment of the white-collar, middle-class workforce did not partake in the tradition of eating out. Rather, the dabbawalla brokered one way to bring the intimacy of home cooking into the work space. In short order, I will delve further into the historical development and nuance of the dabbawalla system, an outgrowth of colonial administrative power in British India. But for the moment, I wish to dwell less on how we might account for the historical emergence of the dabbawalla and hone in on how the figure of the dabbawalla continues to wield cultural power and significance within Mumbai's culinary scape. In particular, the dabbawalla as a figure (beyond his own individual labor) enacts a kind of dexterous labor that is appealing on many levels—culturally, socially, and politically. More than simply delivering food from domestic spaces to work spaces, this form of public food entrepreneurship appeals to different aesthetic and political sensibilities. This delivery system has the effect of reinscribing gendered scripts of normativity and individual notions of exceptionalism. In a city that has long thrived on its robust food culture, which caters to all palates and to diners of varied income levels, it is almost anachronistic to imagine that a complex food delivery system that brings home-cooked meals from domestic spaces into the urban work milieu continues to thrive despite the ubiquity of public dining options. In a city that has now fully embraced home food delivery via apps like Swiggy and Zomato, India's successful counterparts to Grubhub and Uber Eats, we are at an interesting cultural moment to rethink the forms of intimacy that have been brokered by one of the city's longest-standing delivery services that is known for relying on predigital forms of food delivery through which food travels from the home to the workplace rather than from restaurants to the home.

As someone who grew up visiting family in the suburbs of Mumbai in the 1980s, I was used to seeing dabbawallas but paid little attention to them amid the other modes of conveyance fighting to inch forward in Mumbai's fabled traffic. During the 1980s and 1990s, the dabbawalla merely functioned as a laborer who worked to make ends meet within Mumbai's public spaces. The dabbawalla could often be seen either on a bicycle with dozens of dabbas in tow, precariously making his way through Mumbai's infamous traffic, or rushing through platforms on the suburban railway lines, balancing atop his head a large wooden crate overflowing with dabbas.

In recent cultural history writ large, the dabbawalla has become a repository of tradition strategically repurposed to signify different cultural and economic meanings within a new neoliberal India. At a moment when the nation is celebrating all the ways in which it has not only entered but fully embraced (and in some cases ushered in) the digital age, *The Lunchbox* stands apart as a film that is resolutely critical of the ways in which technology and the digital are imagined to make the world smaller, facilitate communication, and broker intimacy. At the same time that the dabbawalla is being remade into an emblem of a new and efficient India, he is also lauded for his ability to broker intimacies by relying exclusively on seemingly outmoded forms of technology and infrastructure. Within the past quarter century the dabbawalla has become an iconic figure who has been co-opted into different cultural narratives in order to signal Mumbai's emergence as a global cosmopolitan city. In 2017, for instance, the city of Mumbai unveiled a thirteen-foot-tall statue, "Dabbawalla," designed by artist and sculptor Valay Shende. Occupying a prominent location in the affluent South Mumbai neighborhood of Tardeo, the statue is made of discarded wristwatch dials. For Shende, the use of this material is one way to chronicle the narratives of punctuality that are central to how the dabbawalla's labor is imagined.[3]

As a cultural critic, I am particularly interested in the kinds of narratives that emerge about the dabbawalla and the particular purchase this iconic image has had globally in networks of public culture. *The Lunchbox* remains the most well circulated cultural narrative about the dabbawalla among both national and global audiences. *The Lunchbox* is unique among the extant body of cultural texts about dabbawallas that intriguingly poses the question of how we might broker new ideas about intimacy if the system that is celebrated for being infallible can produce new and perhaps heretofore unimaginable connections among strangers while also upending narratives of neoliberal multiculturalism. Unsurprisingly, then, in addition to Shende's statue, the image of the dabbawalla is also widely available in other cultural venues.

The Indian artist Bose Krishnamachari, for instance, has been creating large-scale installations built around the centrality and iconic value of the dabba. His multimedia installation *Ghost/Transmemoir* is a complex installation that debuted in 2003 and has traveled to several museums around the world. In 2008, I was able to see it in person at the Peabody Essex Museum in Salem, Massachusetts. A rather massive undertaking, the work is about forty feet long and includes dabbas that were previously used by the dabbawallas of Mumbai. The installation, which at first glance looks like a tangle of wires, headphones, and metal, consists of hundreds of dabbas mounted on iron scaffolding. Within each dabba is a small LCD monitor. Museumgoers can walk up to the piece, put on a pair of headphones, and watch a range of interviews that play on the various screens.

According to Krishnamachari, his mixed-media installation deliberately uses the dabbas because of their iconic status in circuits of Mumbai's public culture. He notes, "the LCD monitors kept inside the boxes that project interviews with a range of Mumbai residents—from street vendors to socialites, industrialists and intellectuals, give a kaleidoscopic view of the city and various facets of its life: displacement, joy, dejection, etc. It gives the viewer a different perspective of the city."[4] As noted in the description in the museum catalogue, "the idea is to capture the city's chaos and disorder, and a constant battle that involves varied experiences like balancing on the scaffoldings of high-rise buildings and travelling on the omnipresent local trains. The installation gives viewers a feel of the city life that unfolds."[5] Certainly, as I navigated through the installation, I noticed how it made clear that the dabbas served to contain the multitude of stories of people who live in the city. Yet the visual appearance of a messy entanglement of wires, headphones, metal creates a somewhat dissonant experience that nevertheless results in a developing sense that the dabba contains scores of stories—many of which are unheard and unseen. And in viewers, a certain kind of curiosity develops as to what more these narratives contain. What intimate details of the dabbawallas' lives and stories do not spill over from the screen or the dabba and into our minds?

Subodh Gupta, another contemporary South Asian artist, has also used the dabbas in his installations. In *Faith Matters*, developed between 2007 and 2008, Gupta creates a piece that consists of a table atop which several dabbas are arranged. On the table, several dabbas made of stainless steel are placed in close proximity so as to "resemble a typical skyline."[6] In one version of the installation that I saw at the Museum für Moderne Kunst in Frankfurt, Germany, in 2014, the dabbas were placed atop a sushi conveyor belt and moved continuously across the table. Per the accompanying brochure for this exhibit, "the installation alludes to the system used . . . for delivering lunch to office workers." As the dabbas travel around the table on the sushi conveyor belt, one senses the constant motion of the object, perhaps recalling for some the way the dabbas move through the public spaces of Mumbai—on trains, on bicycles, and on foot. The circular motion of the dabbas around the conveyor belt reminds us of the loop each dabba makes each day. It travels through space, from home to workplace, but it eventually returns to its starting point, only to then make the trip again the next day. It is a slow motion, but a methodical one, signaling to the calming but constant circulation of the dabba within this makeshift cityscape.[7]

More recently, the comic book artist Abhijeet Kini released a short comic book titled *Dabbawala: Feeding Mumbai since 1890*. Almost functioning as a primer of sorts, the ten-page comic book briefly rehearses the history and story of Mumbai's dabbawallas. Asked to complete an oral presentation on superheroes, a young boy, Avi, implores his parents for help on his assignment. His parents suggest that instead of looking to caped heroes, he should consider the role of the dabbawalla, an everyday superhero in Mumbai. Although primarily didactic in function, Kini's comic nevertheless positions the dabbawalla as an everyday hero for doing necessary but undercompensated labor.

And although the references remain rather sparse, Salman Rushdie alludes to the vital cultural work that the dabbawalla does in the imagination of Mumbai in his controversial novel *The Satanic Verses*. Quoted in the epigraph to this chapter, Rushdie notably imagines the possibility of failure, an idea that is almost universally repudiated in the stories of dabbawallas.

Finally, the story of the dabbawalla would not be complete without attention to the role the dabbawallas themselves play in shaping their image in circuits of public culture. Cognizant of the cultural capital their story wields, dabbawallas—particularly those in managerial positions within the largest of the dabbawalla collectives—have the potential to wield significant cultural power in shaping the narrative about the singularly spectacular performance of the dabbawalla as an example of Mumbai's economic acuity.

I mention all of these forms of cultural work—art installations, novels, comic books, and statues—to drive home the point that the dabbawalla enjoys a rather unusual level of visibility in circuits of public culture. To this end, I argue that the dabbawalla bears the freight of the long cultural history of public forms of dining in Mumbai, but that its image has also done much to articulate a particular narrative of modernity about the city such that the system of dabbawallas has evolved from being seen mostly as a form of public dining that functions at the "utilitarian level of daily necessity"[8]—and has functioned as such since the city's emergence as a colonial commercial and industrial center in the early nineteenth century—to an idea that defines the aesthetic of the city. Visual artist Bose Krishnamachari notes that the reason for the popularity of this iconography is obvious: "*Dabbawalas* are intrinsically associated with the city's culture, with the masses. Plus the novelty value, as they are unusual to our cityscape."[9] I suggest, however, that the connection is anything but intrinsic. Rather, the dabbawalla was specifically propelled into attention on the global stage by a deliberate marketing strategy that rested heavily on recasting the terms of a story published in the pages of *Forbes* magazine. As Mithila Mehta notes, "ever since they were thrust into the limelight with a six sigma gradation, the dabbawalas have become an omnipresent, almost overused metaphor for the city's dynamism."[10] Part of my argument will be an exploration of how the apocryphal stories surrounding the Six Sigma gradation helped propel the dabbawalla into the global spotlight. At the same time, I also consider how the dabbawalla, though a convenient and appealing metaphor through which to explore the uneven textures of everyday life in the global city, can also contain other narratives that are not so easily explained by the neoliberal narratives of corporate efficiency that are at the heart of the national story of success about the dabbawallas that is being exported. To this end, I argue that the work of cultural producers like Ritesh Batra radically puncture the narrative of the dabbawalla by emphasizing the sociality and networks that can be brokered via predigital forms of intimacy, thereby offering a reconceptualization of what the dabbawalla signifies culturally and politically in a globalized India. The dabbawalla is imagined as a figure of success and an image of the efficient economic structures of a modern and globalized Mumbai. But alongside this narrative, another emerges. Ultimately, *The Lunchbox* is invested in drawing out certain truths about gender and intimacy by casting the true story of the dabbawalla into a fictive light and by imagining the possible lines of connection enabled by predigital forms of networking that draw people in the city together.

Dabbawallas and the Gendered Labor of the Supply Chain

How do the dabbawallahs, a group of lowly educated Indians from the Pune region, build a world class distribution system to solve this delivery problem?
—Balakrishnan and Teo, "Mumbai Tiffin (Dabba) Express"

Before I enter more fully into a discussion of how *The Lunchbox* creates intimate eating publics, it is worth exploring the historical emergence of the tiffin box delivery system and how it came to play such an important role in the image of Mumbai as a modern city, despite the fact that the system of dabbawallas includes only some five thousand workers and only serves a small portion of Mumbai's 12.5 million inhabitants. The word *dabbawalla* is a portmanteau derived from Marathi words and literally means "lunchbox-man."[11] This network of dabbawallas, ubiquitous in their signature white caps and outfits, has been providing an essential service to office workers in the city for more than a century. Early in the workday, a dabbawalla collects in a dabba, alternatively known as a tiffin box, home-prepared food from domestic residences.[12] Following an elaborate system of delivery and exchange that is wholly reliant on travel by bicycle, on foot, or via the system of suburban railways, the dabbawallas transport the lunchboxes to a central sorting place, where they are sorted once again before being transported to the desks of office workers in the city. Around 2:00 p.m., the entire journey is reversed and the dabbawalla returns the tiffin box to the home from which it was picked up earlier that day. Each day, close to 175,000 dabbas are transported in this manner throughout the city of Mumbai.[13]

As Frank Conlon notes, this system of food delivery "offers an inexpensive and 'homely' alternative to taking lunch in a restaurant by providing home-prepared food from residences."[14] But what were the initial reasons for the need for this kind of lunch service? As Conlon notes, the demand for a lunch delivery service grew out of the particular demands of the British colonial administrative system and the changes wrought by the imposition of British workday timing. Whereas members of India's educated, male middle class in Mumbai were used to eating a large midday meal at home before going to their offices, which opened around 10:30 or 11:00 a.m. and allowed them to refrain from eating food prepared outside the home, both the imposition of new work hours and the physical growth of the city "reduced the possibility that most clerical workers could consume all meals at home."[15] In lieu of carrying a lunchbox to work amid the throngs of commuters, the largely male white-collar workforce could opt into a system that allowed them the privilege of maintaining their dietary preferences for the cost of three hundred rupees a month, while also allowing the gendered ideology of the wife being the preparer of meals to remain intact. Although few studies have explored the invisible labor that women perform to make these meals possible (their work must be completed each day by 7:00 a.m., when the dabbawalla arrives), several studies have explored how a labor force has emerged in the city of Mumbai to serve the needs of the predominantly male, middle-class workforce.

As feminist scholars of social reproduction theory have noted, women's labor within the home is often undervalued or invisible. Tithi Bhattacharya notes, one understanding of "social reproduction is that it is about two separate spaces and two separate processes of production: the economic and the social— often understood as the workplace and home."[16] Building on these ideas and honing in on meal preparation as a central aspect of how social reproduction occurs within the home, Farha Ternikar notes that this kind of work can be understood as the "second shift" South Asian women engage in. After working a full day, women come home to undertake yet more work. This kind of labor, Ternikar notes, is often invisible and "often materializes as additional grocery shopping and provisioning as well as extra time in the kitchen and [at] the dinner table."[17] The contexts of the COVID-19 pandemic have made it all too clear that domestic work is an undertheorized and unacknowledged site of labor (largely because the labor performed does not count as "productive" in the sense of contributing to standard economic measures), but food studies has long acknowledged that cooking is a form of labor that occurs within the domestic space.

One of the few academic studies on the dabbawallas is curiously silent on the issue of gender. Although the author, Uma Krishnan, is acutely aware of the class dynamics at play, she goes so far as to praise the dabbawalla system. Quoting Raghunath Medge, who notes that men in conventional heteronormative marriages "don't want to inconvenience the ladies of the household, mother or sister or wife, to wake up early in the morning to make lunch for them,"[18] Krishnan nonetheless does not reflect on the fact that marital privilege allows men to expect that a meal will be prepared for them by the women in the family. Indeed, the great innovation of the dabbawalla delivery system is that it merely makes the intimate labor of meal preparation less inconvenient, even as the work of meal preparation remains intact.

Historically, the system of dabbawallas dates back to the late 1890s; it was started by Mahadu Havji Bache, an immigrant to Mumbai from the *taluka* (district) of Rajgurunagar in Maharashtra. To meet the demand of the Indians working for the British administrators, he recruited men from his taluka. Eventually, the dabbawallas formed an organization called the Nutan Tiffin Box Suppliers Charity Trust, which is still operational today. The highly visible public face of the organization, Raghunath Medge, has been the primary architect behind what Gauri Pathak describes as the "Orientalized image [of the dabbawallas] as simple, unsophisticated people" that has become so pervasive in circuits of public culture.[19]

The dabbawallas use a delivery system that has been widely lauded for its efficiency and ability to work with the existing infrastructure of the city (figure 1.1). Pathak describes the delivery system thus: "The delivery process is a complex one, carried out efficiently without the aid of advanced communications of information technology. Lunchboxes are all marked with basic symbols that code their origin and destination. Each dabba changes hand about four times one-way, yet there's no specialized divisions of labor and every dabbawalla is involved in the entire supply chain. Daily about 175,000 lunches are accurately delivered by individuals who traverse the entire length of Mumbai relying only on the coded symbols for addresses"[20] (figure 1.2).

Scholars of supply chain management and food writers alike have marveled at the ingenuity of this system and have often discussed at length the challenges that emerge from transporting meals from a wide geographic area into a relatively narrow slice of the city. As Natarajan Balakrishnan and Chung-Piaw Teo note, the "system operates using a zoning system approach. Each zone is served by a team of 20–25 dabbawallahs, each serving around 30 customers per day. Each team operates as a separate business unit, and the team leader (called mukadam) is responsible for the efficient coordinated functioning of the team."[21] They also describe the unique ways in which the system works with the apparent limitations of having a semi-illiterate workforce:

The dabbawallahs chose to evolve a coding system that "speaks" to its bunch of illiterate workers, fully recognizing the fact that its strength lies on its cheap labour and committed workforce. The code, which is painted on the dabba top, is restricted first by the size of the top itself— 6 [inches] in diameter. The code uses colour, dashes, crosses, dots and

Figure 1.1 Photo of a dabbawalla and his tiffin boxes on his bike in Mumbai. Photo credit: Joe Zachs from Pune, India, 2007. From Wikimedia Commons, reprinted under CC BY 2.0 license, https://creativecommons.org/licenses/by/2.0.

Figure 1.2 The marking system used on dabbas. Photo credit: Jonathan Silbermann from Berlin–Schöneberg, Germany. From Wikimedia Commons, reprinted under CC BY-SA 2.0 license, https://creativecommons.org/licenses/by-sa/2.0.

simple symbols to indicate the various parameters like originating sub-urb, route to take, destination-station, whose responsibility, the street, building, floor et al. The system by its simple structure ensures a smooth flow to and from destination.[22]

They are laudatory in their praise for the efficiency of this model, but their rhetoric is replete with classist and Orientalist assumptions. As noted in the epigraph to this section of the chapter, also drawn from Balakrishnan and Teo's article, they marvel at the fact that an illiterate and little-educated work-force has so ably created such a world-class distribution system.

This image of the exceptionally illiterate subject who has transformed models of efficiency has become part and parcel of how the dabbawalla is packaged for the world. Absent from the characterization of the dabbawallas as illiterate is any recognition of their unique literacy practices. Brian Street, for instance, notes that it is vital to "make visible the complexity of local, everyday community literacy practices" as a means of challenging myopic understandings of culture rooted in a stereotypical understanding of culture.[23] Building on Street's work, Uma Krishnan's study of the literacy practices of dabbawallas reveals a complex form of literacy that has developed over years. As she notes, the dabbawallas rely on a complex multilingual script to enable the massive undertaking that is the accurate system of food delivery across Mumbai. Al-though imagined as conventionally illiterate, the dabbawallas, Krishnan notes, learn to read and write the English alphabet in order to facilitate doing their jobs. Part of becoming an experienced dabbawalla involves "writing the codes using letters, numbers and colors [as] part of their everyday routine[, which] over time . . . [leads] to mastery."[24] As Krishnan's ethnographic study reveals, it is problematic to cast the dabbawallas as simple and uneducated folk who have overcome all odds to create a complex and efficient supply chain. Rather, one must become cognizant of the very different ways in which literacy practices emerge and flourish.

Despite being operational since the late 1890s, dabbawallas catapulted onto the world stage only in the late 1990s, when *Forbes* featured them in an article titled "Fast Food." Much has been made of this article in the popular media, but the article only briefly discusses the model of efficiency in the structure of the dabbawalla system of delivery: "And what a process it is—despite the complexity, the 5,000 tiffinwallahs make a mistake only about once every two months, according to Ragunath Medge, 42, president of the Mumbai Tiffin-men's Association. That's one error in every 8 million deliveries, or 16 million if you include the return trip. 'If we made 10 mistakes a month, no one would use our service,' says the craggily handsome Medge."[25]

Of note in the quote above is that *Forbes* doesn't actually claim that the dabbawallas have an infallible system; rather, Subrata Chakravarty, the article's author, quotes Medge and provides *his* statistics. This fact is worth noting because nowhere in the article does Chakravarty mention that the dabbawallas are a Six Sigma company or that the dabbawallas have the Six Sigma certification. Rather, this story is an apocryphal one that has seized the public imagination and continues to circulate as a part of the narrative about the dabbawalla. Chakravarty notes that Six Sigma is a process that refers to a level of efficient operations and that no such certification exists, yet the *Forbes* story continues to be repeated and quoted even in purportedly official and peer-reviewed monographs and articles about dabbawallas. And perhaps most importantly, Medge, in particular, has been strategic in seizing on this image to repeat this narrative.

The Intimacy of Failure in *The Lunchbox*

Ila: The lunchbox went to someone else.
Deshpande Aunty: But the deliverymen never make a mistake.
—*The Lunchbox*

As scholars such as Jacques Derrida, Linda Kauffman, Janet Altman, and Hamid Naficy have noted, epistolarity involves multiple acts through which receiving and sending letters are involved. Naficy notes, "epistolarity involves acts of sending and receiving, losing and finding and writing and reading letters. It also involves the acts, events, and institutions that facilitate, hinder or prohibit such acts and events."[26] Particularly intriguing in Naficy's assessment of epistolarity is the role that letters play in mediating distance. He writes, "exile and epistolarity are constitutively linked because both are derived by distance, separation, absence and loss and by the desire to bridge the multiple gaps."[27] Ritesh Batra's film *The Lunchbox* emerged as a surprising hit in late 2013; for a while there was even discussion that it may have become a contender for India's official nomination to the Oscar foreign film award. Batra's *Lunchbox* is one of the only feature-length films to structure its story around the failure of the dabbawalla system. What if, the film seems to ask, the dabbawalla system is not as infallible as it is imagined to be? And what if, amid this new fallible structure, an intimacy is created among an unlikely pair of characters who might have never crossed paths? This form of stranger intimacy emerges in *The Lunchbox* through the exchange of letters. When a lunchbox is delivered to the wrong address, Saajan Fernandes, an office worker, receives the unintended epistle (the meal) and responds in kind by sending his own epistle—in his case, a letter written in English. When the errors continue over the series of weeks, the epistles continue. Ila sends her culinary messages in the form of delicious meals packed into a tiffin, accompanied by a letter written in Marathi, and Saajan sends back an empty dabba with his own epistle written in English. Through this serendipitous error, these two strangers build a relationship that develops entirely through the exchange of written and culinary epistles. It is worth noting, however, that the figure of the dabbawalla is a subaltern figure of sorts, quickly shuttled into the background of the film, a point I will return to later in this chapter. As the film moves forward it gestures toward the kinds of productive intimacies that emerge in the spaces in which human error and fallibility fail to secure the kinds of intimacies that the dabbawalla system is designed to broker.

Within the current system that the neoliberal economic models of efficiency celebrate, the dabbawalla is the invisible laborer who transports hot, homemade meals from the domestic space to the workplace each day. His value as a laborer is only apparent if he can properly facilitate an exchange of food, a culinary message of intimacy between family members that refuses failure. But might there be another way to read Batra's film, rather than as simply a romance that merely uses the potential of the dabbawalla failure as a backdrop to its narrative. What if the film can be read as more than a "*what if the process failed*" narrative? Jack Halberstam notes for instance that "we might read *failure*, for example, as a refusal of mastery, a critique of the intuitive connections within capitalism between success and profit, and as a counterhegemonic discourse of losing."[28] Following Jack Halberstam's lead, I suggest that the idea of failure opens up an important critical perspective from which understand the critique of modern familiality and intimacy as it emerges in this film. Halberstam provocatively asks, "What kind of reward can failure offer us? Perhaps most obviously, failure allows us to escape the punishing norms that discipline behavior and manage human development with the goal of delivering us from unruly childhoods to orderly and predictable adulthoods."[29] Of note here is the idea that a system that embraces failure can produce unexpected and pleasurable spaces of reprieve from systems that expect routinized forms of behavior, both between and among family members and in corporate work spaces. In *The Lunchbox*, the dabbawalla's failure allows Ila, an unhappy housewife, to undo the violent banality of her everyday life. With a deep focus on the visual, the film trains its focus on the spectacularly beautiful meals that Ila prepares every day for the tiffin box while also unmasking how deeply unhappy her everyday life feels to her.

Relatedly, the failure allows Saajan to experience a form of intimacy, a human connection that he has not had in the many years since his wife passed away. When he suddenly begins to receive the lunchbox, his daily ritual of going to the office, meticulously churning out reports, and returning to an empty house is jolted out of its routines and regularity. Saajan, all of a sudden, has something to look forward to at work beyond fulfilling an obligation to his employer; his sense of self-worth is not tied to being a productive worker. Rather, he anticipates the moment of failure each day when the wrong dabba will arrive and he can look forward to receiving a letter from Ila, someone he has never met. Without a failure in the system, there is no possibility for an intimacy to develop. And it is precisely in that momentary escape from the everyday, the ability to inhabit another space, another possibility, that his affective horizon is charged differently.

Part and parcel of acts of epistolarity is the ability to bridge seemingly impossible distances. As Janet Altman notes, "to write a letter is to map one's coordinates—temporal, spatial, emotional, intellectual—in order to tell someone else where one is located at a particular time and how far one has traveled since the last writing."[30] In each letter, Saajan and Ila effectively draw a map of their own location, be it emotional or intellectual. In each letter, Saajan and Ila make clear how much closer they have come toward establishing a new intimacy that is not bound by the strictures of a conventional heteronormative arrangement. To be clear, neither Saajan nor Ila seems interested in pursuing a sexual affair. Rather, their intimacy is about sharing their worlds, having someone to talk to and having someone with whom to share the ups and downs of quotidian life. To be sure, the romance feels sweet, though not saccharine, because it is about the affective intimacy brokered by the simple act of exchanging letters and food. Neither Saajan nor Ila is able to or wants to eat with each other. Instead, they are buoyed by the possibility that writing letters to one another allows.

Ultimately, *The Lunchbox* is structured around a series of failures that paradoxically highlight the importance of labor within the domestic familial space. When the film begins, Ila the unhappy housewife can be seen painstakingly preparing a meal to be dispatched via dabbawalla service to her emotionally unavailable husband (figure 1.3). A figure who seems always to lurk

Figure 1.3 Film still from *The Lunchbox*, depicting Ila preparing lunch to be delivered by dabbawallas.

in the background, Ila's husband appears permanently tethered to his phone. Whether he is texting or glancing furtively at his phone, he is seen as a character who is wholly not present. And yet, Ila remains resolutely committed to trying to gain his attention. But without this glitch in an otherwise perfect system, there can be no reprieve from her life and the largely hidden nature of her labor. By highlighting the failures that are possible within the system, then, Batra's film also renders visible the other forms of labor that largely go unmarked within the dabbawalla system of exchange. So much of the film is focused on the interior spaces of Ila's home, particularly her kitchen. We see how she prepares meals, has conversations with her neighbor, and that these small gestures, focused on the everyday, are where she derives most of her sense of self and value as a human being. Ila does not even leave the space of the apartment until the second half of the film.

Consider, for instance, how the audience learns about the mix-up that sets the film's intrigue into motion. At the beginning of the film, a series of quick shots depicts Ila juggling the many tasks of being a stay-at-home mother. She rushes to get her daughter ready for school, to prepare hot rotis on the stove, to fill the dabba with rice, while also soliciting advice from Deshpande Aunty, her upstairs neighbor who relies on a sense of smell to tell her what Ila needs to do to improve the taste of her meals. At the same time, Ila looks out of her tiny galley kitchen to see the dabbawalla ride up on his bicycle to pick up the meal. She rushes to finish filling the dabba as she hears the insistent doorbell. A wordless exchange ensues as she hands over the dabba to the dabbawalla. As he rides off in the rain and the lunchbox starts to make its way through the city, we see a momentary flash of Ila's unhappiness as she remains moored in the kitchen within the confines of her apartment.

In the sequence that follows, we see how the food travels from Ila's kitchen to Saajan's desk. Although one short sequence focuses on the dabbawallas' system of delivery and their movement through the public spaces of Mumbai, the real intrigue comes from seeing Ila, and later Saajan, in their everyday space. The film alternates between their points of view. In the film, the first indication that something is amiss is when the dabba comes back empty. Aware that her husband does not usually eat the meals she prepares, Ila says, "It's like he's licked it clean," to which Deshpande Aunty upstairs says, "This is a new beginning." When Ila's husband returns and refuses to return Ila's gestures of everyday intimacy and can only respond to her question, "How was lunch today?" with the bland response, "It was good, your alu gobi was really good," Ila realizes there was a mix-up. She had not prepared alu gobi, but green beans.

At this stage in the film, however, it is not clear how her husband ended up with a meal of potato and cauliflower curry instead of the green beans she had cooked. The error is explained in the next scene, when Saajan stops in at the restaurant delivery service that usually sends in his meals and compliments the service for the exceptionally good meal. The restaurant worker seems perplexed as to why Saajan would compliment the otherwise staid meal, but he tells his coworker, "The alu gobi did it for us." At this moment it becomes clear that an error occurred in the dabba delivery system. Saajan had received the dabba of home-cooked food that contained the delectable green beans that Ila had prepared, while her husband had received the restaurant-made potato and cauliflower dish. Moreover, the audience may be privy to the productive failure and to the unexpected and welcome form of intimacy that occurs between Ila and Saajan, but the dabbawalla himself is wholly unaware of his role in enabling this intimacy. Indeed, to some extent the film suggests that the nameless working-class dabbawalla's life remains unaltered even as he has played such an important role in changing the lives, however temporarily, of these two middle-class characters. The dabbawalla serves as little more than a plot device, thus suggesting that his value derives from brokering middle-class intimacies, whether or not they adhere to the strictures of marital fidelity.

When the error is repeated the next day, Ila also includes a written epistle in the dabba. She writes, "Thank you for sending back an empty lunch box. I had made that food for my husband. And when it came back empty I thought he would say something to me. For a few hours I really thought the way to the heart was through the stomach. In return for those hours I am sending you paneer. My husband's favorite." As Saajan reads the letter, the scene cuts back to Ila's home, and the camera trains our eye on Ila's labor.[31] In particular, it focuses on the tactile, luscious, and intimate nature of making food. We see the care with which Ila prepares this meal, the time she takes to slice vegetables, roll paneer, and mix ingredients. The intimacy of her labor comes through vividly and is a visual counterpart to the letter that she has written and the food that Saajan, someone she has never met, is eating in an office somewhere she's never been. In this way, the film accesses an alternative narrative about labor—that of the woman in the kitchen who each day prepares hot meals, often before the day has even fully begun.

Her labor is given a space to emerge and is presented in visually lush and thoughtful terms throughout the film. Through these moments of cooking for someone whom she imagines eats and enjoys her food, her labor becomes valued; indeed, it is through a failure of this infallible system that the largely invisible labor of someone like Ila becomes visible and valued within a system that does not ascribe value to the kind of labor that is a form of intimate care. But I also suggest that there is more to this failure, particularly when we notice how it morphs into a form of desire that allows Ila a far greater degree of agency. If we attend more to the issue of gender, we see that the protagonists in this film—Ila and Saajan—feed a hunger that exists within each of them. Ila, quite rightly, is dissatisfied with her marriage and absent husband, who actively prefers the generic meals prepared by an outside vendor over the meals lovingly prepared by his wife. From the very beginning of the film, Ila is all too aware that her husband is emotionally unavailable to her. His refusal of intimacy is made apparent by his constant tether to his mobile phone; ostensibly he is always working, but it is also plausible (and even suggested) that he is having an extramarital affair with someone with whom he communicates via texts.

Despite efforts to put herself into her cooking and to woo her husband back through food, he has no idea about (or apparent regard for) how invested she is in their marriage. Indeed, it is with the help of her upstairs neighbor, Mrs. Deshpande, who never appears on screen but rather is a disembodied or acousmatic voice, that Ila develops an elaborate plan to woo her husband via her culinary prowess.[32] As Muzna Rahman notes, "Ila attempts to use the culturally mandated tools at her disposal to reaffirm her and her husband's heteronormative roles within the respectable Indian family";[33] and yet the irony is that he pays no attention to the quality of the food, even preferring a mass-produced meal to her home-cooked one. As Mrs. Deshpande notes: "Rajeev ate someone else's cooking yesterday and he didn't even notice!" The implicit critique that emerges at this point is that connections to digital and mobile technologies do not necessarily enable communication or better intimacies. Community and real connections, the film seems to suggest, emerge when strangers come into proximity with one another despite the fact that they are never supposed to meet. The dabbawalla system, wedded as it is to narratives of perfection, is intended to maintain the workings of heteronormative marriage. Despite and against modernity's incursions, a largely invisible workforce will labor efficiently to ensure that wives can continue to cook for their husbands.

The film, however, accesses an entirely different narrative, one that would lay bare the utter abjection that a woman like Ila feels until her life is shaken up by this felicitous error. A notable scene in the film reveals how Ila feels trapped by her domestic existence; most of the shots in the film show her confined to the small apartment. Often the space is dimly lit, adding to the sense of confinement. For Ila, the only way she knows to win her husband back is to rely on the tools that gendered scripts have made available to her. To recapture the sense of intimacy that has long since disappeared from their marriage, she cooks for him, trying to re-create domesticity in a sense, thereby reminding him that she is the kind of wife who is attuned to her spouse's needs. But when the dabbawalla system breaks down, the two protagonists who never meet in the movie each nourish the appetites of the other; they offer each other a much-sought-after intimacy that takes the form of food production and consumption. As a traditional homemaker and woman, Ila is charged with upholding and reproducing good citizens. As I argued in my earlier book, "the home, never a neutral space divested of ideological constructions of gendered nationhood, is a site that produces gendered citizens of the nation."[34] Ila, in a sense, performs her ideological role of being a good wife and mother; her daily activities center around caregiving.

As the film unfolds, Ila and Saajan's relationship continues to grow through the kinds of dishes Ila prepares and through the letters they exchange, in which Saajan provides feedback about the quality of the food. Arguably, what makes their alimentary relationship so intimate over time is not that Saajan unflinchingly loves every meal Ila prepares. Rather, he assumes a form of intimacy whereby he tells her when the food is too salty or too spicy. When they initially begin exchanging notes, Saajan responds to Ila's first letter with an all too taciturn response: "Ila, the meal was very salty today." In response, Ila prepares the next meal with an extra dose of chilies. Perhaps Saajan notices the latent meaning behind this gesture but his letter only notes, "Dear Ila, the salt was fine today. The chili was a bit on the higher side. But I had two bananas after lunch. They helped to extinguish the fire in my mouth. And I think it'll also be good for the motions."

A still camera focuses on Ila in the kitchen, as she reads the note and furrows her brow in confusion because of Saajan's apparent refusal to engage with the message she tried to send—*criticize my food and I'll burn you*. Saajan's note instead recontextualizes her efforts and delves into the most intimate part of eating, the abject. From here, the meals continue, but the letters take a marked turn to the intimate. From discussing the nature of the food, the conversation turns to the seemingly mundane details about their everyday lives. The upstairs neighbor who is confined to his bed and stares at his ceiling fan all day; the painting Saajan buys on his way home; listening to old cassettes; the crowded trains; tales of Saajan's endearingly annoying coworker; watching old TV shows that Saajan's wife had recorded—little things, seemingly. Nonetheless these are intimate details that Saajan and Ila can share only with one another. Ila's husband is too busy with other things to talk to his wife, and Saajan, as a widower, is shut out of a world connected to more normative forms of belongings. As he puts it, "I think we forget things if we have no one to tell them to." In this way, Saajan and Ila become the caretakers of each other's memories and stories.

But they also remain tethered to a nostalgic version of the past that is pretechnological. Their intimacy is brokered via letter writing and home cooking. They discuss their fondness for music on old cassettes. They may live in a rapidly modernizing city of the Global South, but their hearts remain firmly anchored in a nostalgic, predigital version of the past. Although they never meet in person and the film quite deliberately refuses us the narrative satisfaction of providing definitive closure to their story, it emphasizes that life is about the small gestures of the everyday. In the end, we return to our daily spaces of living, to our kitchens; we make rotis, we talk to our neighbors, who don't always see us for the people we are; we steal outside for a few moments to have a cigarette and watch neighbors eat their evening meal before they notice us looking and draw the curtains. And we write letters to strangers who do see us for who we are, even without meeting us in person, and who might, as Saajan wistfully notes, for a moment, let another person into their dreams.

Part of the appeal of a film like *The Lunchbox* is that it imagines what it may look like to cook and eat alone but not be alone. Through the many exchanges of letters and food, intimacy is built between the two main characters, two unlikely people whose paths never cross. Although Saajan and Ila arrange to meet at a restaurant, when Saajan shows up at the restaurant and is confronted by the fact that he is much older than Ila, he decides not to let her know he is at the restaurant. Earlier in the day, Saajan offhandedly catches a glimpse of himself in the mirror and is reminded of how much older he appears. It is this image that haunts him when he sees a much younger Ila at a table, seemingly hopeful about the possibility of meeting the person with whom she has formed an indelible intimacy. Ila sits at a table, unaware of his presence, wondering why he has not shown up. Later, perhaps understandably feeling jilted by this unintentional betrayal, Ila sends Saajan an empty lunchbox (figure 1.4). In his letter to Ila, Saajan writes, "I got the lunchbox today, there was nothing in it, and I deserve that. Yesterday you waited in the restaurant for a long time . . . I came to the restaurant while you were waiting, fidgeting with your purse, drinking all that water. I wanted to come up to you and tell this all in person, but I just watched you wait. You looked beautiful, you are young, you

Figure 1.4 Film still from *The Lunchbox*, depicting the empty dabbas Ila sends to Saajan.

can dream and for some time you let me into your dreams and I want to thank you for that."

Although their conversations continue, their relationship effectively ends on this heart-wrenching note. Ila sends Saajan only one more letter intimating she will move to Bhutan with her daughter, harkening back to an earlier letter in which she had revealed an interest in the possibility of moving to Bhutan: "Yashni told me that in school, she learned that in Bhutan everyone is happy. There is no GDP there. They have Gross National Happiness." Despite the melancholic tone to Saajan's and Ila's final letters to one another, the ending of the film is not necessarily unhappy simply because they do not end up together on screen. The film nudges us toward thinking that each character has found a way to be alone and to even enjoy the possibility of solo communion. The intimacy that Ila and Saajan sought with a stranger functions as a temporary respite from their loneliness. And yet it is telling that at no point does the film position normativity via coupling with a more loving and present partner as a way out of their current loneliness brought about by a cheating or deceased spouse. There is no happily ever after for either character. But there is no unhappily ever after either. The kind of unmitigated happiness that would merely replace one loving individual (Saajan) for an unloving spouse is not presented as a viable or desirable outcome.

At the end of the film, Saajan retires and goes so far as to return to his hometown of Nasik. His retirement is temporary, however, and he returns soon thereafter to Mumbai, to his home, to his balcony, and to his life, and the film even offers a brief glimpse of him riding the train with a group of dabbawallas. All of this transpires without Ila's knowledge; in letting go of his past, he has also let go of the brief intimacy with Ila. And, in keeping with the theme of missed encounters, Ila—unaware that Saajan has left his office job—shows up at his place of work only to find that he is not there. Ila, we are led to believe, concludes that this means he has left Mumbai for good.

The film ends with Ila and her daughter entering a taxi: it is unclear whether she is headed to Saajan's house or to her own home, or if she is finally moving to Bhutan in search of a country that values "gross national happiness" over "gross domestic product." In her final letter to Saajan, Ila had noted that she sold her jewelry and was preparing for the move to Bhutan. She explained that she would send the letter to him in Nasik, or perhaps she would keep it for herself and read it again sometime in the future. Although we don't actually know what happens, it is clear that, as Rey Chow notes, "their contact loop is forever broken—the delivery of lunchboxes has terminated with Saajan's retirement. . . . We realize that Ila's writing voice has, in fact, been cast into the void."[35]

The link between the two, as Chow suggests, is severed forever, but I suggest that this ending is not actually a form of closure. Rather, the film does not allow nor require that kind of closure and leaves us in this moment in medias res—we don't know whether Ila will go to Bhutan or return to her flat in Mumbai. But ultimately, it does not matter. By the end of the film it is clear that although Ila and Saajan may have momentarily staved off their loneliness, their temporary but intense intimacy allowed them to understand that being alone is not the same as being lonely. In their embrace of solitude, they become queer creatures. In their acceptance of solitude, they refuse to invest emotionally in the promise of heteronormativity as the only way to render life bearable. Rather, they find ways to be alone and to thrive, even if only temporarily. The alternative temporality of their liaison suggests that there is more to the "good life" than marriage or the promise of fidelity. Even after their spouses die or cheat on them, life goes on. And perhaps more poignantly, the film does not judge either character for creating an intimacy that would flaunt marital conventions; rather, it suggests that intimacy comes in many forms and marriage is no guarantee that happiness will accompany it. The good life, for both Ila and Saajan, is not necessarily about making a home together but about being at home where they are, however temporarily. Through food, and through the sharing of letters, each finds a form of affectively fulfilling intimacy—however fleeting it might be.

Loneliness, once a borderline experience usually suffered in certain marginal social conditions like old age, has become an everyday experience of the ever-growing masses of our century.
—Hannah Arendt, *The Origins of Totalitarianism*

The only thing considered worse than eating alone has been eating alone in public.
—Stephanie Rosenbloom, *Alone Time*

Feeling nervous about your reservation for one? Bring a book if you must, but resist the urge to stay glued to your phone or catch up on work. The point of dining solo is to enjoy some quality time with *you*—not your to-do list.
—Alyssa Schwartz

As I discuss in the previous chapter, part of the appeal of a film like *The Lunch-box* is that it imagines what it may look like to cook and eat alone, but not be alone. Through the many exchanges of letters and food, two unlikely people, whose paths never cross, build intimacy. As I move from thinking about forms of intimacy with strangers (where strangers commune over food though they never meet in person) to examining texts where the individual eats alone but may be looked at or gazed upon by strangers, it is useful to evoke Hannah Arendt's mediation on the difference between solitude, isolation, and loneliness. In "Ideology and Terror," Hannah Arendt develops a tripartite structure for understanding how the condition of being lonely, isolated, or alone can feed the mechanisms of totalitarianism. Speaking of and to her experiences living under the Nazi regime during the 1930s and 1940s, "Ideology and Terror" isolates three forms of being alone: isolation (*Isolation*), loneliness (*Verlassenheit*), and solitude (*Einsamkeit*).

For Arendt, the very structure of isolation is a threat to political life. "Totalitarian governments," she notes, "like all tyrannies, certainly could not exist without destroying the public realm of life, that is, without destroying, by isolating men, their political capacities. But totalitarian domination as a form of government is new in that it is not content with this isolation and destroys private life as well."[1] By taking away the human capacity to have contact in the public sphere, by destroying the human ability to form intimacy, by isolating human beings from one another, totalitarian governments could come into existence. This isolation, Arendt notes, is not the same as loneliness (*Verlassenheit*). Loneliness, in some ways, has far more pernicious effects because of its ability to destroy individuals' intimate and interior lives. As Arendt puts it, "loneliness is at the same time contrary to the basic requirements of the human condition and one of the fundamental experiences of every human life. Even the experience of the materially and sensually given world depends upon my being in contact with other men, upon our common sense which regulates and controls all other senses and without which each of us would be enclosed in his own particularity of sense data which in themselves are unreliable and treacherous."[2] Put another way, only in creating intimate ties with others can one experience the world. To be lonely is to be uprooted, unmoored, and unrecognized by others.

To inhabit the space of solitude (*Einsamkeit*), however, is something entirely different. Per Arendt: "In solitude, in other words, I am 'by myself,' together with myself, and therefore two-in-one, whereas in loneliness I am actually one, deserted by all others. All thinking, strictly speaking, is done in solitude and is a dialogue between me and myself; but this dialogue of the two-in-one does not lose contact with the world of my fellow-men because they are represented in the self with whom I lead the dialogue of thought."[3] As she puts it, there are "various ways in which human singularity articulates and actualizes itself."[4] Solitude, Arendt clarifies, is not about being alone and stands in contradistinction to loneliness and isolation.[5] Rather, "I can be very bored and lonely in the midst of a crowd, but not in actual solitude, that is, in my own company or together with a friend, the sense of another self. That is why it is much harder to bear being alone in a crowd than in solitude."[6] The capacity to feel comfortable in solitude is less about being lonely than about being at home with one's self. Unlike isolation and loneliness, solitude allows for creative thinking and activity to flourish. For Arendt, when in a space or state of solitude, one can make the kinds of moral distinctions that one cannot make when isolated or lonely.

As discussed in the previous chapter, both Saajan and Ila, the protagonists in *The Lunchbox*, come to this realization; in solitude, they may not be in the company of one another but they have communion and intimacy. Without a necessary attachment to another person, an *other*, they are still able to feel content in their solitude, without descending into an abyss of isolation or loneliness, or assuming that normativity will take away their sense of loneliness. Only through the act of crafting culinary intimacy does either learn to navigate the space of solitude.

And yet for all intents and purposes, characters like Ila and Saajan appear to be profoundly lonely. Arendt's useful designation between isolation, loneliness, and solitude helps add nuance to cultural understandings of what it means to occupy the space of solitude; further, it helps to elucidate how and why we need to think carefully about solitude as a condition of possibility and not simply of loss and absence. As a case in point, it is worth examining how the fact of solitude is often mapped onto experiences of loneliness and isolation. Although ample evidence suggests that race, class, age, and ability might exacerbate feelings of marginalization among any of the aforementioned categories of aloneness, it is equally the case that those who might find themselves alone are also those who might be considered queer. Here, I am taking a page from Michael Cobb's incisive analysis of singledom in *Single: Arguments for the Uncoupled*. For Cobb, Arendt also provides a useful point of entry into understanding why being single is considered so terrible. He writes, "part of the reason being single is terrible is that it's been made into a mystifying condition, marked by failure, characterized by an almost unassimilable oddity despite its always threatening ubiquity."[7] I will return later in this chapter to the point about failure, but for the moment it is worth noting how and why Cobb's understanding of the single as a queer and reviled figure also draws inspiration from Arendt's musings on being alone. Cobb explains: "It might sound odd that I would start thinking about totalitarianism's origins and the socio-psychological effects of terror as one method to think about the plight of the single. But if my queer theory training has taught me anything, it is that I should be vigilant about the rhetoric and politics of connection, especially intimate connection. And if there's no intimacy, no intimate connection, then what can one think?"[8]

Cobb seizes on an important point in Arendt's musings on aloneness. Notably, he makes clear how intimacy and intimate connections are structured by how we think about both rhetorical and political connections. For Arendt, the isolated individual is vulnerable to the apparent lure of totalitarianism precisely because they desire intimacy but are seemingly unable to form those bonds that keep solitary individuals from becoming lonely. But as Cobb makes clear, the rhetorical terms we use to describe the conditions of being solitary or alone also structure how we think about intimacy. Accessing a vocabulary or rhetoric of loneliness is vitally important in shaping how we contour our understanding of intimacy outside of a framework of normativity. It is with this idea about giving shape to the notion that intimacy can be usefully rethought via the lens of the figure of the single (following Cobb) and solitude (following Arendt) that this chapter attempts to work through multiple significations of eating alone and the construction of intimacy. In articulating intimacy with solitude and the act of eating, I focus primarily on two cultural sites: a series of photographs by Miho Aikawa, and a scene about a woman eating alone from the novel *Bodies in Motion* by Sri Lankan American author Mary Anne Mohanraj.

Food, Labor, and Normativity

Heteronormativity, the family, and eating are always inextricably linked. Food studies in particular has worked to make visible the often-invisible forms of labor that cooking and meal preparation take. Although this work of documenting the invisible labor practices of women is vital for any kind of feminist project, it is also important to take stock of the underlying assumptions that structure the significant attempts to make visible this kind of labor within the home—something that, as discussed in chapter 1, has been a central tenet of social reproduction theory.

To wit, within the past decade, a wide corpus of writing about food in the home—particularly in diasporic contexts—has emerged within ethnic studies and its interlocutory fields of gender, race, and sexuality studies. One such work is Krishnendu Ray's *The Migrant's Table*, a sociological inquiry that maps the foodways of Bengali American households in the United States. Through a series of interviews and thick ethnographic research, Ray establishes the central desires and ideas at stake within the Bengali American culinary imaginary. But implicit in his analysis, as with several inquiries into foodways in the domestic space, is the notion that food preparation within the home is yoked to an unyielding form of heteronormativity. At the same time that his thick ethnographic work makes visible the work women do in the kitchen, noting in particular how women seek to reinforce or bring their own spin to Bengali home cooking, cooks within the home are almost always described in Ray's work as "wives" and "mothers," such that South Asian diasporic foodways are mapped by an implicit heteronormativity defined by a familial tethering to a couple or family. And yet the home space is one of the least likely spaces to guarantee what I refer to as unyielding heteronormativity. The kitchen is often already a homosocial space that allows articulations of same-sex intimacy to emerge through and against the strictures of a regimented kind of heteronormativity. Culinary narratives are particularly rich sites for examining the queer potentialities and the promises of desire precisely because food preparation within the domestic space is heavily invested in the ideologies of heteronormativity. When cooking is about the queer, and when cooking refuses the narrative of unequivocal happiness, it establishes alternative logics. If cooking is resignified in order to complicate heteronormativity, it can become about pleasure—not teleologically oriented toward a "happily ever after" that often implicitly circumscribes a narrative of heteronormativity, but about an alternative kind of affective fulfillment that understands pleasure without insisting on happiness or a happily ever after.

Embedded in this narrative about eating together with families and loved ones is an aspirational ethos. We eat together to establish connections among loved ones. We eat together to establish forms of intimacy and to avoid being alone. Sitting together around a table is a way for people to be convivial. Under the constant pressure of securing access to the "good life" is the implicit notion that normative ways of being in and moving through the world (primarily as a couple) are how to establish meaningful forms of intimacy. Under such circumstances, the success embedded in being a good subject is measured by one's ability to be part of this kind of unit wherein social value is secured by attachment to familiar units such as the couple or the family. Moreover, this ideal, under conditions of neoliberal multiculturalism, reminds us of the aspirational quality of this lifestyle. Even as one may, on occasion, eat alone or without a partner or without a family, one should almost compulsively desire this kind of arrangement, orienting one's desires toward a future goal of togetherness. But as this chapter suggests, we would do well to flip the script and consider the myriad ways in which intimacy and happiness are not always yoked to the idea of being among others. Imagining intimacy in other forms, particularly through the act of solo dining, is also a way to access alternative visions of gender and sexuality—ones in which new possibilities for intimacy and queer subjectivities emerge when women choose to eat alone in public or semipublic spaces, even as and when these kinds of possibilities often seem unimaginable or impossible.

In her pathbreaking work on queer diasporas and South Asian public cultures, cultural critic Gayatri Gopinath theorizes the position of impossibility vis-à-vis the articulation of a queer female subjectivity. For Gopinath, the "foregrounding of queer female diasporic subjectivity is not simply an attempt to bring into visibility or recognition a heretofore invisible subject."[9] Female solo diners, I suggest, unwittingly inhabit the space of this kind of impossibility. The queer subject is always already an impossible subject within the context of a heteropatriarchal structure that delegitimizes queer female subjectivity. In my own life, I have noticed a disjunction between, on one hand, the implicit mandate to always orient oneself toward eating with others and, on the other, the strong desire I possess to become at ease with eating alone.

To turn for a moment to my own experiences with being and becoming alone, I want to discuss anecdotally my own journey into the world of single eating. In December 2017 my partner of almost twelve years left me. It was painful and emotionally difficult, and it came with all the attendant issues that come with the end of a relationship that has defined more than a decade of one's life. After two months of a steady diet of coffee, kombucha, and yogurt, leaving the house only to go to work, I had to check myself. One of the first things I did was force myself to go out to and eat in public spaces. Alone. And I didn't just go to Panera or Starbucks; I chose sit-down restaurants where someone would bring me a menu. I chose food from the menu and ate a three-course meal. It was during those meals that I realized that even when I was coupled, I spent many years traveling alone for work and pleasure. Eating alone was not new. What was new was feeling I had become a character in a Radclyffe Hall novel and would forever dwell in my well of loneliness. During those many trips, I also found myself wanting or needing to eat alone. And yet unwittingly, after decoupling, I inserted myself into the script of how a solo woman diner should exist within the public space of a restaurant designed to broker intimacy among couples, families, and other recognizably normative units.

So, I often did what many solo eaters do and what Alyssa Schwartz, in the epigraph at the beginning of this chapter, suggests women should do. I brought two crucial accessories: a cell phone and a book. Because to have a book or a phone is to signal to the rest of the world that you are self-possessed and do not feel abject. To orient your experience of eating while also being tethered to a recognizable object that connects you to alternate realities and temporalities secures your place in normative space and time. The fact that I maintain a strong social media presence around food means that I post photos of many of my meals to the photo-based social media site Instagram. Taking pictures of beautifully plated food is my way of also making the experience of solo dining less solitary. I share the images with my carefully curated community of "followers," who then share their experience of enjoyment via affirming notes, expressions of envy, and comments about shared feelings about the pleasures of the palate. The possibility of accessing a different spatiotemporal locality via the sharing of a picture of food is one way to broker intimacy. My friends may not be with me physically as I eat, but they are with me in the afterlife of the meal.

I have now made a habit of eating alone at several restaurants. Over the course of two vacations in 2018, I solo ate my way through Bali, Indonesia; Rome, Italy; and Bangalore, India. The irony of choosing the same countries that Elizabeth Gilbert picked during her solo travels, and which she later chronicled in her best-selling *Eat, Pray, Love* (discussed in a later chapter), was not lost on me. Yet there was little about any of those experiences that, for me, rotated around the idea of seeking spiritual fulfillment—or even worse, love. Quite simply, I wanted to enjoy being able to eat meals in public spaces without the attendant shame that comes with the idea of being a hypervisible solo diner. What was remarkable about this experience is that I was insistent about not being seated at a bar but getting a table of my own. In my own way, I was queering the dining experience by being comfortable asking for a table for one. The bar, after all, is often where wayward solo diners are relegated. I certainly enjoy a good meal at a bar, but I also do not like to be made to feel less than. Or that I must unyieldingly accept that as a solo diner, my provenance is at the bar, perched on an uncomfortable backless stool, sitting as a lonely person among a crowd.

The act of eating in restaurants is also a way to lay claim to making the public space feel intimate for a certain period of time. Certainly restaurants and restaurant designers often think about ways to create intimacy via the design of the space. In an article for *The Atlantic* titled "Creating Public Intimacy: Designing Restaurant Booths and Banquettes," architect David Rockwell discusses how in his line of work he must think about ways to create a sense of intimacy within the public space of a restaurant. He notes that the ways people sit in groups, inhabit space, behave, and make eye contact are all directly affected by the seating configuration throughout the room. In other words, the forms of social engagement within restaurants are almost always contingent on how tables are arranged: Are there booths? Banquettes? Spaces for communal dining? Of note in his article is the idea that "the booth actually created a room within a room, private space for two, three, or four people."[10] It is worth reiterating that his concept of creating intimacy is predicated around a social unit that comprises two to four people. The booth allows friends and loved ones to create a form of intimacy. But, one might ask, what does booth dining afford the solo diner, who may alternatively seek privacy via the booth or a form of stranger intimacy by sitting in a less protected environment at an open table or at the bar? Rockwell's inability to imagine a space for the solo diner is not unusual; simply put, most restaurateurs are not necessarily invested in the solo diner, despite the fact that—if we are to believe the results of a recent study by OpenTable (the extensive restaurant reservation system)—reservations for solo dining have grown by 85 percent since 2015.

And yet when one thinks about eating, one thinks about the conviviality of the eating experience. It is not only about what one eats—though in my case what I eat is often what is primarily important—but with whom and where one eats. So, one might ask, how do we work through the anxiety that seems to undergird the idea of women eating out alone? As early as 1964, celebrated food writer Craig Claiborne discussed this subject. In an article titled "Dining Alone Can Pose Problem for a Woman," he notes that "some New York restaurants are reluctant to accept unescorted women during the dinner hour."[11] He goes on to share anecdotes about ways that women have been successful in gaining reservations for solo dining. He applauds one particular diner for her approach, which he describes as both "naïve" and "ingenious," but he also notes that numerous women do not know how to manage it.[12] Curiously, perhaps the problem stems not from women seeking to eat alone at lunch, but at dinner. One woman he discusses in his article notes that there is "not a place in town where a woman can't dine alone if she knows how to manage it."[13] Claiborne came back to this topic many times, persuading New York Times readers that eating alone did not have to be a chore.

Without ascribing an overly teleological narrative of feminist progress (we are better now than we were in the past), one may forgive readers in 1964 for thinking women should not eat out alone. One cannot, however, grant the same lapse in imagination for a restaurant that is less than accommodating of solo female diners in 2019. In January 2019 the Manhattan restaurant Nello came under fire for essentially refusing to seat a solo female diner. In an essay titled "The Night I Was Mistaken for a Call Girl," Clementine Crawford, a regular patron of the restaurant, describes a particularly ugly incident. Describing a visit to a restaurant she had frequented for years—choosing to sit at the bar alone—she remarks on being asked to sit at a table instead, while a male diner was allowed to remain seated at the bar. She writes: "Why, I wondered, was I suddenly being treated so frostily? Surely, in America of all places, the customer was still king—or, in this case, queen? After further interrogation, it transpired that the owner had ordered a crackdown on hookers: the free-range escorts who roamed the Upper East Side, hunting prey in his establishment."[14]

In other words, the restaurant had deemed that any solo female diner was potentially a sex worker. Apart from the obviously sexist and misogynist implications of suggesting that sex workers should be hidden from view, the restaurant also automatically coded Crawford as a sexual object. She continues: "So when doing an optics inventory on their patrons they treated the single woman in a patriarchal fashion: they automatically objectified, sexualised, put her (me) in a box—the treasure chest of pleasure. Would a man on a business trip, or one who routinely ate alone, have attracted the same attention and treatment? Well, no: clearly not, because, as I saw, they served him."[15] Crawford's words perfectly capture the widespread anxiety about eating alone. As I read her narrative, I find that my task as a cultural critic invested in thinking about the narratives that script how we inhabit the public and semipublic spheres converges on the optics of eating alone. It is all too easy to say, "It's just me. I don't feel comfortable eating alone." But what if we press this logic to think about how we are often socialized to think that eating in public spaces comes with particular demands and desires for normativity? In particular, why does this social stigma so often focus on the ocular—the sense that one is being looked at, that one's choices are being surveilled and scrutinized? To be sure, one of the dynamics that makes solo dining fascinating is not necessarily whether people are actually looking askance at solo diners but the anxiety that comes from the imagined freight of being an object that is looked at, pitied, and jeered. How might looking at visually oriented works that teach us to look differently allow us a different point of entry into understanding what it means to eat alone?

As a first step in situating the solo diner as a kind of queer figure, I stage a conversation between two radically different cultural objects. The first is a series of photographs titled *Dinner in New York* and *Dinner in Tokyo* by Miho Aikawa. The second is an arrestingly beautiful scene from the novel *Bodies in Motion* by Sri Lankan American author Mary Anne Mohanraj. I juxtapose these two cultural objects because of the ways in which they train us to reorient our gaze on the solo diner. What if, instead of seeing isolation and a lack of happiness, we see scenes of solo eating as profound acts of intimacy that are brokered by a radically different relationship between the diner and their meal?

"Table for Two, or Just You?"

In a series of twenty-four beautifully composed photos, photographer Miho Aikawa captures diners as they are eating dinner. In several of the photos—seventeen, to be exact—Aikawa photographs people eating alone. The settings range from eating on a train, at the workplace, at home—in bed, in front of the TV, or with a laptop—or at a restaurant. In each photograph we see a solitary figure in the middle of their meal. Their faces display neither happiness nor unhappiness. They are often focused on the act of eating—looking at their food, taking a bite out of a sandwich, slurping noodles. On occasion, their gaze is directed to another object such as a laptop, TV, or desktop screen. The people are of all ethnicities, races, and ages. They are variously clad in comfortable clothes, work attire, or pajamas. In her artist statement, Aikawa writes: "I have no intent on saying that having dinner with a cell phone is bad and eating alone is sad. My idea of this project is to propose what dinner is to people, how different it can be for everyone, and [to] present the diversity found in this everyday act. When you enjoy mealtimes, you're more likely to eat better."[16] With each photo, Aikawa invites us to see both the pleasure and the intimacy of eating alone. These aren't the kinds of scenes of unbridled happiness that are propagated by the now-famous series of memes titled "Women Laughing Alone with Salad." In an article of the same name, Edith Zimmerman constructs a picture essay in which we see a series of stock photos of nineteen thin and mostly white women who seem to derive complete joy from eating salad.[17] In contrast to Aikawa's photographs, nothing about the texture of everyday life is captured in these meme-able photos. What is actually being sold is a kind of aspirational version of happiness. Fitting into an ideal of womanhood means not only eating your salad but laughing when you do so. The perfect, happy woman loves her salad, is thin, and relishes that she can move through the world without feeling guilt. These women want to eat what they are supposed to eat, and they are unquestioningly happy—even elated—that they get to eat their iceberg lettuce and anemic tomatoes.

By contrast, Aikawa's photos traffic in no such idea of happiness or healthfulness. The people in her photographs simply are. They eat. They live their everyday lives. Each photograph's focus on the intimate setting of a meal unmasks the ways in which eating is a part of the texture of everyday life. And yet while viewing these pictures, the viewer establishes a moment of intimacy with these diners. We are not voyeurs, but we glimpse how they eat and how they move through the world. In the image in figure 2.1 we see a young woman, barefoot in her kitchen, caught in medias res as she is eating a strand of pasta. The caption tells us, "Queenie loves to cook simple dinners at home like pasta, and enjoys taking the time to relax." The image conveys a sense of stillness. Queenie is not ecstatic about her meal. She is simply partaking in an act she enjoys—eating a meal that she has prepared for herself.

A photo from the *Dining in Tokyo* series captures a woman also in the middle of a bite (figure 2.2). The artist notes, "Sawako Okuhata lives in an apartment by herself and usually has a quiet dinner in the dining room, but when she is too exhausted, she has a light meal on the bed, watching TV." There is a simplicity to the everydayness of this moment—she sits at her dining table, with a place setting laid out for her, and enjoys her meal. The image, like the others in the series, is quiet and almost wholly unremarkable. At heart, the series also tells stories about the lives of people in urban spaces. By placing these domestic scenes in public view, these photographs create an intimacy among diners who eat alone at home and those who eat alone in restaurants or at the workplace.

All of Aikawa's photos have an unhurried quality about them. Whether the subject is someone like Zheng Yun, a fifty-two-year-old woman who lives with her children but usually eats dinner alone, or like twenty-nine-year-old Kazumi Kaneko, who we see eating a salad (notably not laughing) and drinking a beer, we see women who cleave out a space to eat a meal without apparent regard for how they are being looked at. In looking at these photos, I kept asking myself what drew me to them. Part of it was seeing gendered and racialized bodies taking pleasure in eating alone. As Bakirathi Mani notes, when we look at photographs we often "establish a mimetic relationship of identity to the visual object in order to claim the image as an affirmation of ourselves."[18] Mani goes on to complicate the function of photography, what the viewer sees, and how racialized subjects' invisibility in circuits of public culture can lead us to cathect these images. These "claims to the photograph as proof of our belonging" operate in different ways for viewers and in tandem with the vision an artist—in this case like Aikawa—is trying to bring to life.[19] For me, the desire to find myself in these photos resonated strongly with Mani's powerful assessment of the dynamic exchange that occurs between the viewer, the photograph, and the artist. What Mani describes as diasporic mimesis, "the bind[ing] together of images that appear to represent the lived experience of

Figure 2.1 "Queenie loves to cook simple dinners at home like pasta, and enjoys taking the time to relax. Age: 32 Time: 7:27 p.m. Location: East Village, New York." Photograph from *Dinner in NY*. Photo credit: Miho Aikawa.

Figure 2.2 "Sawako Okuhata lives in an apartment by herself and usually has a quiet dinner in the dining room, but when she is too exhausted, she has a light meal on the bed, watching TV. Age: 54 Time: 7:13 p.m. Location: Itabashi-ku [Japan]." Photograph from *Dinner in Tokyo*. Photo credit: Miho Aikawa.

racialized subjects, with the viewer[']s desire to be represented in the public sphere as a racialized immigrant,"[20] so profoundly captures the desire of the viewer and the experience of looking at photos. As I looked at these photos again and again, it became clear that I wanted to see images of women like myself, women of color, eating alone. In this sense Aikawa's photos resonate so strongly for viewers like me because of the ways in which they so deftly capture the idea that eating is an unhurried act to be enjoyed and not judged. Collectively, the photos capture the quiet moments of pleasurable solo intimacy that each diner carves out for herself.

The Queer Erotics of Eating Alone

But what if we consider eating alone to be about more than a form of isolation? What if we extend the narrative of solo dining pleasure to think about the possible underlying erotics of cooking and eating? Notably, must eating alone always suggest that one is excluded from the possibilities, pleasures, and erotics that emerge from sharing a meal? To examine this, I turn now to a work that deliberately unsettles the idea that an erotics of eating can emerge only from the normative structure of a couple sharing a meal. I wish to explore what it might mean to think about the erotics of eating when one is a solo diner. There is, of course, a long tradition of erotically charged images of women eating. In 2009, the Indian American host of *Top Chef*, Padma Lakshmi, famously appeared in a commercial devouring a Hardee's Thickburger.[21] As she sits on the stoop of a building, her legs slightly akimbo, the camera focuses our gaze on Lakshmi slowly and seductively eating her burger. As the sauce drips, she licks it clean. Announcing that she has always had a love affair with food, Lakshmi in this advertisement reveals how much she revels in the experience of not just eating but devouring a meaty burger. This advertisement is arguably the definition of food pornography, but if we look at it another way, it is—to be sure—for the male gaze, but it is also a sort of celebration of the female eater who will gleefully eat something other than a salad and revel in the fact that people are watching her. The pleasure in this moment comes from the knowledge that she is eating alone but also that this intimate moment is very much in the public eye. The gustatory gaze that falls on Lakshmi is as much about watching her as it is about realizing that this moment is one of intimacy between a woman and her burger. It is in the pleasure of seeing and being seen that this scene from the advertisement acquires legibility.

The erotically charged novel *Bodies in Motion*, by Sri Lankan American author Mary Anne Mohanraj, is one in which perfection and coupling are elusively presented as something that, though possible, are not always the ultimate goal. A spinster who appears in two chapters of the novel refuses a narrative of compulsory heterosexuality within the kitchen. In the first instance, I use the term *refuse* to signal a rejection in favor of alternative epistemologies. In the second instance, I use it to signify a re-fusing of ideology, one that creates a different kind of assemblage to negotiate the heterotopic space of the kitchen.

Mary Anne Mohanraj's *Bodies in Motion*, a multigenerational novel spanning several decades of the twentieth century, chronicles the stories of two extended families and their lives in Sri Lanka, Britain, and the United States. In Mohanraj's novel, the possibility of inhabiting queerness is enabled by the workings of the culinary. Through a series of interlocking stories spanning the more than six decades from 1939 to 2002, Mohanraj's novel weaves the stories of two families, the Vallipurams and the Kandiahs. In their search for a place to feel at home in the world, the characters in Mohanraj's novel continually negotiate the vicissitudes of immigration, war, and displacement that impact their everyday lives. From the outset, the heterosexual seams that stitch together the tapestry of this sprawling extended family are carefully unraveled. Through the course of the novel, marriage rarely acts as a guarantor of unyielding heteronormativity. Instead, moments of queerness gently chip away at the edifice of heterosexuality around which the architecture of familial life is built.

One such narrative emerges through the character Mangai Vallipuram, a woman who remains unmarried into her old age. Mangai's story, like that of most of the characters in this novel, occupies little space within the larger narrative; only two distinct vignettes among the twenty that make up the novel specifically focus on Mangai. Introduced in the chapter titled "Seven Cups of Water," her story is completed in the epilogue "Monsoon Day." We first encounter her character in 1948, when Mangai is seventeen. We then learn about the rest of the members of the two families and do not encounter Mangai again within the narrative for another forty-eight years, when she is sixty-five years old. Spatially, the novel makes an analogous move: whereas Mangai is first introduced in the northern city of Jaffna, Sri Lanka, the final section takes place in Colombo. From the chapter in which her character is first introduced, Mangai is marked as a queer subject. In the early days of the marriage between Mangai's brother, Sundar, and his new wife, Sushila,

Sushila finds herself unfulfilled affectively and sexually by her husband. She thirsts for intimacy, and each night after the household goes to sleep, she enters the kitchen in search of water to quench that desire. During a week's time, the exchange of water between Mangai and Sushila becomes decidedly more erotically charged, moving from a literal embodiment of thirst to a more figuratively rendered one. Mangai describes the intimacy of sharing water as follows: "I picked up the cup, raised it to my lips. I filled my mouth with water, soaking the dry roof of my parched tongue. I turned to face her, still enclosed in the circle of her arms. I leaned forward, placed my lips on hers, and gave her water. She sucked the water deep down her throat, swallowed, and I felt the motion in my lips, making each mouthful smaller and smaller, each transfer taking longer and longer, until the cup was not just empty, but dry."[22]

Sushila might be able to slake her own thirst, but Mangai feeds her sexual appetite, such that it quickly becomes apparent that these clandestine nightly encounters soon begin to work through and against the implicit heteronormative logic of the domestic culinary space. When slaking thirst alone is not enough to create a queer erotic, Mangai resorts to ever more creative ways to engender thirst. Creating a paste of red chili peppers, she applies the fiery substance to Sushila's body and calms the burning sensations with careful caresses, as water alone is not an effective salve for the incendiary pain. For Mangai, who is intolerant of spicy food, the swirling of chili paste on her tongue combines intense pain and pleasure. "I wanted to suffer for her," she explains, articulating the sting of the pain with the pleasure of intimacy. Although these encounters are short lived—Sushila is resolutely unwilling to leave her husband for Mangai for fear of social censure—they haunt Mangai throughout her life. More importantly, they begin to cleave a space in which to think about the queer potentialities of the kitchen, even as Sushila vehemently forecloses the possibility of entering a visible kind of relationship. Just as the water spills out of the container, so too does queerness spill over the edges of and into the heteronormative home. While Mangai and Sushila never cross paths again, the strategic placement of this vignette early in the narrative—one of the few centered in the kitchen—is important in terms of gesturing toward the queer intimacies enabled through shared palatal preferences.

Although Mangai does not reappear in the novel proper, her story is reintroduced in the epilogue. At this moment the narrative centers on Mangai's weekly ritual, which involves preparing an elaborate meal of rice, fish, leeks, potatoes, and eggs—a meal large enough, Mangai explains, "to feed a man four times her size," but that only she will consume.[23] Mangai's meal, the final one of the novel, in the final scene of the novel, is an elaborate act of producing a kind of culinary perfection that is not about creating a network of care in a conventional sense. She is most decidedly not the kind of maternal caretaker who cooks for the heteronormative family. As she prepares meals each week, she is aware that the neighborhood girls gather around the perimeter of her home, "peer[ing] in through cracks, over windowsills" as she cooks.[24] Despite this voyeuristic surveillance, Mangai "waits until they are settled before she begins to cook. It is another part of the unspoken bargain with her neighbors."[25]

But meal preparation is only part of what makes this moment of gastropornography interesting. As Mangai cooks, she disrobes: as she stirs the potatoes, she undoes the hooks on her sari blouse; while the leeks braise in a pan with turmeric and salt, she unwraps the layers of the sari. She gradually prepares the meal, removing more articles of clothing along the way. By the time her meal is fully prepared, she is completely naked in the kitchen and completely mindful that she has been under the watchful gaze of the children the whole time. At no point are the children ever invited to join her meal, but Mangai performs for them nonetheless. But in the solitary gesture of refusing to cook for children, she refuses to become wedded to an ideological system that deems that women's labor must resolutely engage in a kind of pedagogy—teaching the next generation of wives and cooks to prepare meals for their families. Rather, her pedagogical moves involve inviting a network of girls to contemplate that cooking can be about bodily pleasure and sensual self-affirmation; that cooking is not about becoming good wives to future husbands; that cooking can be about pleasure and communion with the self. The text notes that "Mangai could tell the girl that this kind of cooking is not learned by watching, or even by teaching—that it is only the passage of time that grinds the lessons into the muscles and bones. But she cannot be bothered."[26] In addition to framing cooking as learned bodily knowledge, the absence of caring about how others feel, the disinterest in feeding others she so patently feels, might be understood as part of what makes her a resiliently queer figure. Consider the closing words of the novel:

> When the fish is ready, Mangai turns off the last burner. She takes a plate down from the shelf, battered tin. She fills a tin cup with cold water. She serves herself rice, fish, leeks, potatoes, eggs. There is enough on her plate to feed a man four times her size. She undoes the tie on her underskirt and lets it fall to the floor. Mangai carries the plate and cup

over to the wall; she sits down, cross-legged on the dirt floor, with her naked back against the wall, with the water sliding down, running along her wrinkled skin, over her ribs, pooling in the hollows of her hips. She takes a drink from the cup, and a sharpened edge cuts the corner of her lip. She balances the plate on her bony right knee, and, shuddering with pleasure, she eats.[27]

Although Mangai derives pleasure from this solitary act of eating, one might consider it a form of disaffection, in the terms Martin Manalansan proposes. For Manalansan, disaffection is an alternative mode of domesticity; as he puts it, "it is not resplendent in its heteronormative structurations, but is fraught with the intrusions and intersections of contradictory non-maternal feeling, interests and desires that emerge out of the banal repetitive routines of domestic labor."[28] Mangai resolutely enjoys cooking, but she is not interested in cooking for others. She displays traces of disaffection that inhabit an alternative mode of domesticity insofar that cooking is about making herself happy, not about making others happy in the conventional ways in which women are imagined to be happy homemakers who willingly slave over a hot stove to prepare intricate meals for loved ones. And yet, this space becomes one of female intimacy, but not because Mangai necessarily wishes it to be so. Mohanraj writes:

There are no boys outside, only girls. That is one of the rules, strictly enforced, by the parents, not by Mangai. Only girls outside, to see what they will become in time . . . she brings her neighbors more pleasure as present scandal than she ever could as past expulsion. It is at times like this that they have an excuse to tell her story again . . . . It will give them something to talk about for days. . . . In a way, it's almost a gift she gives them. Perhaps they know it, but she does not do it for them.[29]

Read this way, Mangai ceases to be a pitiable figure or even a cause célèbre for triumphing over adversity and solitude—she is neither unhappy nor happy. Rather than viewing her as a failed subject who falls out of narratives of normative couplehood, I suggest that she is a queer single figure whose everyday demeanor embodies a kind of nonneoliberal resilience precisely because her narrative is not about being happy or unhappy. Her cooking, which, as she puts it, is about "sustain[ing] her in a normal day," positions her as a subject who has managed to overcome various kinds of violence, as a result of her position both as an ethnic Tamil and as a queer woman.[30] Although neither vignette discloses what happens to Mangai in full detail, we learn that during the intervening years spanning the civil war, she was shot, and her neighbors—scandalized by the "woman who had lived with her servant Daya for decades, in a house with only one bed[,] a woman they had insulted, behind her back, and to her face"—left her for dead, bleeding out on the floor of her home, while they looked the other way.[31] She is thus guilty of both being the wrong ethnicity and not being in a conventionally normative relationship. Here we find a re-fusing of what violence looks like—censure against the ethnic body becomes linked to homophobic violence. In either case, Mangai is that queer figure, an assemblage, whose very presence disturbs the community in which she lives. She refuses to allow the failure to enter into couplehood to exile her from the kitchen. Although she may not be a conventional figure, preparing food within the home space to reproduce a kind of culinary nationalism, she does not stop cooking. Indeed, she takes an intense pleasure in cooking only for herself, thus embodying a kind of culinary resilience, because cooking is about making herself happy. According to literary scholar Madelyn Detloff, the concept of resilience stands in opposition to resistance as a mode of engaging trauma. Detloff notes:

> Resilient writing differs from redemptive writing in its refusal to make loss into a metaphor for something else. It diverges from the "unspeakable" hypothesis by recognizing the attempts of survivors to invent, if necessary, new methods of recognizing and communication, without suggesting that those methods are always and only symptoms of trauma's inescapable hold. Another way to describe resilient writing would be to suggest that it respects the dynamic relationships between the particularity of suffering and the temporality of living, of continuing on after, even in the midst of, suffering. Resilience then might be seen as a complex adaptation to traumatic circumstances—but an adaptation that does not "get over" or transcend the past as redemptive narratives imply. Rather, the past, like the "patch," becomes part of the continuously emerging present.[32]

Mangai's affective landscape thus negotiates between a sense of disaffection and resilience: disaffection, because her work is about a kind of queer pleasure that does not simply seek to reproduce culinary subjects in the next generation, and resilience, because she is not interested in being redeemed through her cooking and because she continues to live, even after she negotiates the difficulties of everyday living in a homophobic and xenophobic context. Mohanraj's novel thus resituates the figure of the cook within the home, so that her pedagogical imperative is not about being a wife or mother—or, for that matter, a partner in a coupled situation. In remapping the contours of South Asian foodways, Mohanraj allows for other topographies that are not circumscribed by an implicit heteronormativity. Food indexes queer resilience because it is through and against the act of preparing meals that Mangai, amid this narrative of a sprawling family, gets to have the last word in the novel.

At heart, a startling symmetry is at work in the simultaneous refusal in the works studied in this chapter, investing in perfect communion with another person as an uncomplicated objective. Happiness is not about creating the perfect meal or about eating with loved ones—straight or queer. It is about creating possibilities within spaces that are typically inhospitable to the forms of desire that the characters in these cultural works long for. In the broader cultural context in which these texts operate—the discourse of multiculturalism—there is an expectation of pleasure and joy in the acts of cooking and eating. One expects the act of consumption to be about pleasure. Eating food is about producing happiness. One feels better about difference if one can eat the food of the other. So often, eating is predicated on the notion that the commensal tradition is about celebration and perfect endings. After all, if sharing meals is not about happiness, what, arguably, is the point of commensality and conviviality?

Works like Aikawa's and Mohanraj's unsettle the notion that food must always be narrated within heteronormative frameworks. Within the moments of "failure" are moments of possibility and desire. Beyond the happily ever after lay moments of imperfect delight and failure. To return to Cobb, failure is often connected to being single. Recall his assertion: being single is often considered to be a failure. Singles are looked upon askance because of what Cobb describes as an almost unassimilable oddity. Mangai is undoubtedly an unassimilably odd character. She is threatening to the community because they fear that her lifestyle will be contagious and that the young girls may become like her. She is also a conventional failure because she is a solitary figure. In Arendtian terms, however, she is more of a figure who embraces solitude than one whose life is structured by isolation. By societal standards, she is a failure. But I understand failure here to be more of a generative position within the context that Jack Halberstam describes in *The Queer Art of Failure*. Halberstam notes that "under certain circumstances failing, losing, forgetting, unmaking, undoing, unbecoming, not knowing may in fact offer more creative, more cooperative, more surprising ways of being in the world."[33]

Halberstam's embrace of failure as a condition of possibility helps buoy our understanding of Mangai's queerness and her ability to be in, and her desire for, solitude. Within such a worldview, when the queer subject continues to cook and continues to live, it becomes possible to embrace the queerness of failure and the happily never after, to relish meals that are not perfect but are delightful, and to smile just a little at Mangai's happiness in the face of failure when she declares, "None of those meals came out perfectly—somehow she always managed to ruin them. Secretly, she was glad."[34]

Embracing Failure

Halberstam's embrace of failure stands in sharp contrast to recent shifts by the UK government that simultaneously seek to remove the stigma from feelings of loneliness while also suggesting that loneliness is an issue of national importance. In a surprising move, the UK government, under the aegis of former British Prime Minister Theresa May, created a new government position titled Minister of Loneliness. In a role designed to counterbalance the very real issues stemming from loneliness, the minister—a position initially occupied by Tracey Crouch and in early 2020 by Diana Barran—promises to work against, in the words of May, the "sad reality of modern life and to attend to social and health issues caused by social isolation."[35] Laudable for its efforts to recognize problems of isolation that affect disabled and elderly populations, the ministry nonetheless runs the risk of trivializing a serious issue that stems from a lack of access to proper care for many marginalized populations. Notably, the appointment of Crouch to this position occurred after the Jo Cox Commission on Loneliness released a report on loneliness. The commission was created in order to honor the memory of the Labour MP Jo Cox, who was murdered by Thomas Mair, a right-wing terrorist who vocally opposed Cox's ideas during the Brexit Referendum of 2016.[36] Mair's overt opposition to Cox's anti-Brexit stance perhaps speaks to Arendt's conception of the social perils of isolation. Mair and other white right-wing terrorists are often described as loners—a distinction that is not usually made available to Brown and Black bodies. In no uncertain terms, Mair targeted Cox for believing in a more inclusive vision of Britain.

In this context, it is ironic that the staunchly Conservative Theresa May government would seek to imagine loneliness as a social ill. Notably absent from the press statement issued by 10 Downing Street, and from any press surrounding the creation of the new position, is how the very idea of Brexit and the desire to separate the nation culturally and politically from racial, ethnic, and class difference could resonate with a lonely killer like Mair. Writing in the *New Yorker*, Rebecca Mead cogently calls this logic into question, noting that

> to imagine that a problem as damaging and pervasive as social isolation can be remedied with ample good will and sufficient cups of tea, rather than with a renewed commitment to the kind of institutions that the government continues to undermine, is wishful thinking, as baseless in its own way as the Brexit delusion of restored British independence. Both depend upon fantasy: in the case of Brexit, that a lost sovereignty can be regained without social cost; in the case of the Loneliness Ministry, that a rupture in the social fabric can be repaired on the cheap. Such a separation of costs and effects is impossible: nothing, not even loneliness, happens in isolation.[37]

Of note above is the notion that goodwill on its own cannot remedy the social ills that have been brought about by the UK government's strategic efforts to undo and undermine the very institutions that would seek to find ways to help counter the structural violence that can emerge as a result of isolation.

In my own life I oscillate between coming to terms with the fact that I can be alone, in solitude, and create an intimate eating public without being isolated, and feeling that to eat alone is to endure the worst kind of abjection. I am occasionally reminded of a painting that captured my fancy many years ago and has been described as a work that captures the harshness of solitude. In 2003 I visited the Art Institute of Chicago on a solo visit. During that trip, I stumbled (perhaps late in life for a cultural critic) on Edward Hopper's *Nighthawks*. What captivated me (and continues to captivate me) about that painting is the way in which Hopper captures a sense of what it may feel like to eat alone while in a crowd. In the painting are four solitary figures who do not interact. None of them appear either happy or unhappy. They simply exist. I was drawn to the painting because each viewing produced different affective responses. At times I would feel heart-wrenching sadness at seeing the four isolated figures, going about their own lives, not interacting and seemingly bereft of any kind of intimacy. At other times I would see this painting doing the kind of cultural work I consider many of the works I've written about in this book to be doing—namely, producing an intimate eating public without the mandate for conversation or verbal (or nonverbal) communication. Four solitary figures occupy positions adjacent to one another and consent to a provisional form of intimacy. They do not need words to interact, but they do not exist in isolation. They are part of an eating public comprising four strangers who do not know one another and will likely never cross paths again. And ultimately this message is a seductive one because it speaks so cogently to the kinds of intimacies we all access at one point or another in our lives, when we find ourselves eating alone or eating in the company of others who are also eating alone.

Some years later, I visited the Art Institute again with my then-husband. I walked alone through the galleries and stopped in front of *Nighthawks*. I looked at the painting for several moments, unaware of the people around me. The gallery was uncrowded that day, so I could enjoy my favorite painting in relative solitude. Or so I thought. I later checked social media to find a picture of myself looking at the painting. My then-husband had thought to capture the moment of me communing with my favorite painting and to post it to social media without my permission. In the photo my back is turned to him and I face the painting. I am wearing a white T-shirt and a purple-and-white tasseled scarf. When I saw the photo I was furious. *Nighthawks* is a lovely painting and has been infinitely reproduced on mugs, screensavers, and socks, but it is not the kind of painting that one declares publicly to be their favorite work of art. I was embarrassed that he had captioned the photograph with a note saying, "My wife takes in her favorite painting." More so, however, I was furious that he had taken a picture of a moment of solitary pleasure and shared it with others. I was furious that my intimate moment had become public. What felt most egregious was that this was a moment of intimacy that had been violated. Moreover, it was now an intimate public secret. Everyone knew I loved *Nighthawks*, and my secret fear was that they could also then understand *why* I liked the painting: My fear of being alone. Of eating alone. The happiness I felt seeing this form of stranger intimacy. None of these stories were my own anymore. In fact, so well-known was my love for the painting that my teenage nephews recently gave me a mug with the image of *Nighthawks* on it. And I could trace all of this back to what I perceived as an intimate betrayal by my partner, who thought to share something he thought was beautiful but that felt inviolably intimate to me.

In 2015 I stumbled upon a local art gallery opening. Through the open windows I saw a painting by a local artist, called *After Hopper* (figure 2.3). It was *Nighthawks* with a twist. Instead of four people sitting at a milk bar, it shows four people seated in Skyline Chili, a Cincinnati favorite. Three of the diners are eating a plate of Cincinnati chili. I walked into the gallery, asked the price,

Figure 2.3 *After Hopper* by Robert McFate, 2015. Author's personal collection.

and bought the painting on the spot. When the show closed, my then-husband picked it up from the gallery and hung it on the wall in our living room, across from the couch where I usually sat. He moved out a few years later when we split up, but the painting hung there until I moved out of the house. For a while, the only thing that tethered me to him was the nail he put into the wall to hang the picture. In those last days in the house, in my solitude, I would often look up at the painting and be reminded of the pleasures and possibilities of solo dining, the possibility of stranger intimacy and my own role as a viewer watching people in a painting eat a dish I, too, love.

In my solitude I was never alone when that painting was also present. It did not remind me of my own failed excursion into normativity. If anything, it allowed me to embrace the possibility of failure, solitude, and the possibilities of intimacy for the solo diner. For now, in my new loft, it is stacked on the floor, next to all of my artwork waiting to be affixed to the wall. Perhaps today is the day that I will take a minute to find my toolbox, find a new nail, and hang it on the wall, in view of my dining table, within the space of this new place I now call home.

As I write these words, we are in the second month of the lockdown made necessary by the rapid spread of COVID-19. One of these days, as I sit on one of my beloved slate-gray Eames chairs to eat a meal at my glass dining table, perhaps this painting will buoy me through these interminable days of solo dining that have come to be my mainstay during this period of social distancing. And for a moment, perhaps it will bring a smile to my face to remember that even in solitude—perhaps especially in solitude—there can be pleasure.

Of course I didn't know what a blog was. It was August of 2002. Nobody knew about blogs, except for a few guys like Eric who spent their days using company computers to pursue the zeitgeist.
—Julie Powell, *Julie & Julia*

I'm just gonna come out and say it. *Julie & Julia* is racist. . . . This movie is white, white, white.
—Lawrence Dai, *The Lawrence/Julie and Julia Project*

In 2002, Julie Powell, an unknown government employee, set upon the task of chronicling a culinary journey on her blog hosted at salon.com. The first blog entry, dated August 25, 2002, explains that its author ambitiously proposes to cook her way through Julia Child's classic *Mastering the Art of French Cooking*—all 524 recipes—in the span of 365 days. The culinary journey is framed as a story about "One girl and a crappy outer borough kitchen. How far will it go? We can only wait. And wait. And wait . . . The Julie/Julia Project. Coming soon to a computer terminal near you."[1] One of the most well-known food blogs to emerge during the early 2000s, the *Julie/Julia Project* became the central focus of Julie Powell's 2005 memoir titled *Julie & Julia: 365 Days, 524 Recipes, 1 Tiny Apartment Kitchen—How One Girl Risked Her Marriage, Her Job, and Her Sanity to Master the Art of Living*. Interspersing narratives about the ins and outs of preparing recipes from Child's classic tome on French cooking with fictionalized accounts of Julia Child's life in post–World War II Paris, Powell's text draws its narrative pull from juxtaposing the lives of two seemingly different white women—an unknown food blogger and one of the most well-known culinary personalities of the twentieth century. Seven years later, the story would be repurposed again (this time by Nora Ephron) into the hit film *Julie & Julia* starring Meryl Streep as the indomitable Julia Child and Amy Adams cast in the role of blogger Julie Powell. In addition to developing the screenplay from Powell's narrative, Ephron also drew heavily from Julia Child's memoir *My Life in France* to construct the film's narrative about Julia Child's immersion into the world of food and her subsequent transformation into one of America's most enduring culinary icons.

Although the blog and its subsequent reincarnation as memoir focused more intently on Powell, critical acclaim for Meryl Streep's performance as the larger-than-life Julia Child quickly overshadowed the presence of Amy Adams as Julie Powell, the blogger. Critics would be hard-pressed to find popular or academic analyses that pay attention in any systematic way to the character of Julie. My aim in writing this chapter is not to restore Powell's centrality to this narrative or to unsettle Julia Child's iconic claim to fame. Rather, it is to yield space to a more thorough examination of the complex dynamics that animate this text against the backdrop of what Lisa Nakamura has dubbed digital racial formation.[2] To press Nakamura's point, racial politics are inextricably enmeshed with the cultures of the internet. As such, what does it mean for a white middle-class feminist to use blogging or other forms of online networking to construct a narrative of the self and thereby construct an alternative kind of intimate eating public?

I underscore that blogging, and in particular food blogging, is a kind of intimate eating public insofar as it relies on the blogger to be comfortable creating a public through their own narratives about food, eating, and consumption. For many bloggers who were active during the period when Powell was writing her blog, social media sites such as Facebook and Instagram had yet to develop the kind of purchase they have had for much of the twenty-first century so far. As someone who maintained my own food blog from about 2005 to 2009, where I wrote about restaurants I would frequent in my then home of Columbus, Ohio, and about recipes I would try out at home, blogging was a way to create a living archive of the present. It was a way to write about my experiences with food in what was then a relatively new space for me. It was a way to create a public that included both the friends I had left behind in New England and a way to make new virtual friends out of strangers, none of whom I would ever meet in real life. And despite the public nature of the blog, open and available for anyone to read, it was not something that in my case was necessarily read by a large group of people. Rather, a provisional intimacy emerged through interactions among a select group of people who would visit my blog and add comments for each entry. Although many blogs enjoy far greater circulation than my short-lived foray into this world, blogs like *The Julie/Julia Project* are similarly oriented toward a goal of creating a close-knit public around a particular culinary conceit. In my case, it was writing about food as an East Coast transplant in Ohio who was in search of good and tasty immigrant food. For Julie Powell, it was about creating an online community, an intimate public, around her attempts to cook her way through Julia Child's beloved cookbook. And yet a glance through the archival residues of Powell's blog suggests that her public may not have been terribly active. Few of Powell's entries have any comments, but a public coalesced around the blog when Powell was able to land a book deal chronicling her work as a blogger. Although the blog had created a market, or a public, for her book, what remains in the archive of that moment are not the interactions between Powell and her readers but the book that landed her visibility on a much larger scale than most bloggers achieve.

But the question remains: When a blogger like Powell does not fit the profile of the standard blogger, what does it mean to turn to the internet to find a community of like-minded people? According to the Pew Internet Research Center, bloggers like Powell were not in the majority in the early 2000s, at the peak of blogging. As younger women of color were turning away from traditional blogs to microblogging sites like Twitter, research conducted in 2006 suggested that bloggers, on the whole, were more likely to be women of color younger than age twenty-one than the general population active on the internet.[3]

The explosion of food writing in the 2000s alongside the concomitant rise of the food blog has produced a rich and variegated landscape from which to systematically map the study of internet-based blogs, social media, and other forms of online networking. Although media studies has interrogated the heterogeneous meanings accrued to the construction, dissemination, and consumption of blogs, I argue that certain types of blogging are considered crucial sites of knowledge formation that create an intimate eating public that is facilitated by encounters on the internet. Cultural critic and blogger Minh-Ha Pham notes, for instance, that even though "culture themed blogs comprise nearly 50% of the blogosphere," rarely are they taken seriously.[4] Rather, detractors denigrate blogging about culture as "self-absorbed and superficial, shamelessly open and public," and a "monkey experiment in self-publishing."[5] Pham's inquiry into fashion blogs, those which propel the genre into the sphere of progressive racial politics, establishes important new critical trajectories in terms of thinking about the potentials and limitations of blogging.[6]

Food writers have also expressed widely divergent viewpoints about the relative merit and utility of food blogging. According to Ruth Tobias, author of the food blog *Denveater*, to write without the censure of editors or the dictates of what can conceivably fit on the written page is one of the most compelling reasons to blog about food. The relative freedom of blogging—in terms of not just what to write but also how to construct narratives about food—is a strong motivating factor for blogging.[7] Going beyond the "space time continuum of the printed page," Tobias notes, allows for a renegotiation of what is considered the main story and the supplemental, whereas reader comments allow for dialogue that can potentially shift the contours of "what is merely public and what is truly communal."[8] Leena Trivedi-Grenier, author of the blog *Leenaeats.com*, notes that part of what attracts readers to food blogs stems from the potential to create more dialogue via reader-blogger interaction on blogs: "Food blogs are great at building a feeling of community among their users. Over 83% of participants felt that a food blog builds a better community than print food journalism. Some respondents attributed this to a food blog's comment section, which allows all users and the food blogger to interact and communicate."[9]

Although the cultural legacy of the film *Julie & Julia* has meant that Julie Powell is one of the most well-known food bloggers, she is by no means the only writer to translate her attempts to interface the virtual world of blogging with the visceral world of cooking, thereby creating a novel form of an intimate eating public. Nor for that matter is she the only person to build her credentials in writing via the internet. In what she characterizes alternately as a "yearlong cooking frenzy" and a "simple yearlong cooking lesson," essayist Nani Power turns to digital media to fuel her interest in Indian cooking. Her aptly titled *Ginger and Ganesh: Adventures in Indian Cooking, Culture and Love* chronicles her attempt to learn how to cook Indian food from Indian American home cooks in the suburbs of northern Virginia. Like *Julie & Julia*, the narrative chronicle of this yearlong experiment with food begins online; in Power's case it begins with a short advertisement on Craigslist directed at Indian immigrant and Indian American women, and morphs into an extended meditation on the place of food in the context of whiteness, female domesticity, and American culture. Because of the pointed implications both texts have for thinking about the role of whiteness as fomented through the workings of the culinary, I focus on exploring the racialized implications of both Powell's and Power's use of the internet to access culinary knowledge about the pur-portedly foreign—in Powell's case, French cuisine, and in Power's case, Indian cuisine. Although their writings begin in virtual space, their respective nar-ratives about food have significant implications for understanding the texture of race in the everyday both in the densely populated urban environment of Queens, New York, and the domestic contexts of suburban Washington, DC.

This chapter, then, examines this pair of culinary texts, similarly orga-nized, that turn to digital media in order to build a narrative about a yearlong experiment with food. Although my analysis remains critical of the latent ra-cial implications of each text, I am not denigrating the value of either text or dismissing the potential that either has to articulate female subjectivity through the lens of the culinary. But I take seriously the point that bell hooks makes that consumption is not value or race neutral. As hooks notes, "Within commodity culture, ethnicity becomes spice, seasoning that can liven up a dull dish that is mainstream white culture."[10] In the texts I analyze, avowed femi-nists, whom we might understand as white neoliberal multicultural feminists, use the internet to construct forms of gendered solidarity that ostensibly cross lines of age, race, and class while paradoxically relying on familiar Oriental-ist orthodoxies that marginalize women of color. In effect this type of neolib-eral multicultural feminism betrays a latent anxiety about the position of the middle-class white feminist in the contemporary racial moment.

In this way my work follows on the heels of important work that thinks through the willful act of consumption, particularly in contexts that Jackie Stacey describes as "the taking in of exotic others."[11] Further, the construc-tion of middle-class femininity in these spaces also relies on familiar tropes of centering whiteness within discourses that ostensibly celebrate the embrace of difference. For instance, the anthropologist Ghassan Hage describes the col-lusion between discourses of white multiculturalism and white racism, which work in their own way to contain difference, thus mystifying and keeping "out of public discourse other multicultural realities in which White people are not the overwhelming occupiers of the center of national space."[12]

Any conversation about race must seriously attend to the myriad significa-tions assigned to whiteness. To think of whiteness as solidified against and through what I refer to as Black and Brown spaces is not to merely assume the terms of race that the bloggers implicitly seem to espouse. Rather, the forms of power derived from occupying or dwelling within whiteness while consum-ing otherness are at stake in my analysis. Both Julie's and Nani's quests toward self-improvement are inaugurated on the internet, and they find that their immediate surrounding physical spaces do not orient them toward their desires as they had hoped. Rather, the space of the internet becomes key in orienting them toward desired spaces of dwelling. In the essay "Building Dwelling Thinking," Martin Heidegger makes an important distinction between inhabiting a space and dwelling there. One can inhabit a space, he notes, without dwelling there. To dwell is to stay in place. To dwell is to want to stay in place. To dwell is to be at peace. To dwell is to experience home without feeling unmoored. To dwell, I would add, is also to feel part of a community. Not all buildings, Heidegger suggests, are homes or spaces to dwell. But in common parlance, to dwell is also to fixate on an idea. When one thinks ponderously on a topic, when one dwells on certain topics, one is both in place and in movement. In this case, the body might be in apparent stasis, moored and in place, while the mind is free to travel. Yet for the blogger, dwelling might come to mean something different. As both Tobias and Trivedi-Grenier suggest, blogging enables one to dwell on ideas without fear of taking up too much space on the printed page. Without the constraints of occupying valuable real estate, one can dwell on culinary matters with relative ease.

If to dwell is also to build community, the feature of blogging that allows readers to interact with bloggers also works in service of creating communities. For readers and bloggers to interact is to establish different forms of dwelling that are not necessarily circumscribed by geographical parameters but by the imagined bonds that tie readers and bloggers into a larger community. With this idea of what it might mean to inhabit a physical and geographically bound space while dwelling someplace else—however complicated the implications of that refusal to inhabit and dwell in the same place might be—I now turn my attention to *Julie & Julia*, a narrative that deliberately and strategically uses food to examine the relationship between dwelling, thinking, and cooking.

Cooking with Julie and Julia

Julie & Julia begins by presenting a disaffected Julie Powell intent on finding ways to escape her everyday life in an outer borough of New York City. When she seizes on the idea of cooking her way through Julia Child's classic work on French cooking, it is as much about becoming a better cook as it is about finding strategies to negotiate around the class politics of her everyday. That all of this is set against the backdrop of the immediate aftermath of 9/11 is also relevant. A self-described government drone, Powell works for the Lower

Manhattan Development Corporation (LMDC), an agency she describes as ineffectual; an agency described on its website as "charged with assisting New York City in recovering from the terrorist attacks on the World Trade Center and ensuring the emergence of Lower Manhattan as a strong and vibrant community."[13] Powell's job is to provide a kind of affective care work for families of 9/11 victims, but notably, only families of *acknowledged* victims. The poor and undocumented who were erased from the discourse of 9/11 as a world-altering tragedy are erased from the LMDC's charge and Powell's imagination. Her displeasure at having to do this kind of labor forms the base of her quest to forge an imagined kinship with Julia Child. Blogging about her adventures with French cooking serves the double paradoxical function of distancing herself from the cultural milieu of the community at her doorstep in Queens, while building an online community through her blog.

The narrative is propelled forward by a stubborn desire to create alternative spatial mappings and communities that navigate around excess and the corporeal on one hand, and loss and absence on the other. For Powell, Queens itself is a space that remains unrepresentable except through its excesses and absences. It is both too far away from her life and not sufficiently interesting to sustain living there. To evoke Heidegger, she can inhabit the four walls of her apartment, but it is not a space where she can imagine dwelling. In a revealing moment she describes her frustration with New York life and yearns for a time when she will have access to a more storied life in a less densely packed environment. This future she imagines is a collective dream, shared with her husband Eric and marked by heteronormative aspirations. Sharing a snippet of conversation with her husband, Powell writes, "'Someday,' Eric said, swallowing hard, 'our ship is going to come in. We are going to move out of NY, and we are going to have our house in the country like we've always wanted.'"[14]

Implicitly woven through Eric's promise is an uncompromising view of what we might conceive of as suburban heteronormativity; a house in the country will come to fruition if only she has the patience and good grace to wait out the hard times. That this dream is not achieved during the course of the narrative or subsequently in Powell's life is notable, but more pertinent is the arc of this desire, oriented toward achieving the goal of a future home.

Sara Ahmed's notion of orientation provides a possible point of entry into understanding the importance of theorizing the arc of desire as an act of orientation. Orientation is about negotiating perspectives, to direct oneself toward particular goals and to pursue the correct line of movement. Ahmed notes, "When things are orientated they are facing the right way."[15] To face the right way is to look away from Queens and to orient oneself toward the imagined possibilities of suburban heteronormativity. To be oriented means to know where one's body fits into its surroundings. To be oriented means to know where and how one dwells. Developing Heidegger's line of argumentation, Ahmed suggests that dwelling is not simply to be understood in the spatial sense, as a form of making room, but also in a temporal sense. Orientations thus gesture beyond the immediate moment and location. They are also directional, guiding one to what is ahead.

In Powell's narrative, to be in Queens, specifically Long Island City, is to be without direction. It is to be unmoored. And to be a nonimmigrant in a space that is home to immigrants is also, ultimately, to be out of place. Throughout, the text narrates an anxiety about living in an outer borough. Powell continually laments that her social life is marred by her distance from the main through lines of the affluent, young, urban, white class that is comfortably lodged in the West Village, appropriately distanced not only from the bridge-and-tunnel populations of New Jersey and the outer boroughs, but also from the racial and class diversity that characterize these spaces. Strikingly, Powell's narrative is shot through with strands of a sheer determinism to do what she seems to consider undoable: prepare French food in all its complexities in one of the presumably least likely spaces, a "crappy kitchen," as she calls it, in Long Island City in Queens instead of Paris, and in an unlikely time—2002, not 1961.

From the outset Powell makes it clear that part of her foolhardiness stems from trying to achieve the impossible while she is living in Queens. In contrast to Julia Child's location in the idyllic culinary center of 1960s Paris, her version of her reality and its perceived lack is exemplified when Powell arrives at "Recipe 58 and Day 36" of the project, which involves preparing steak with beef marrow sauce.[16] She posits her frustration with her location, both temporal and spatial, as follows: "I did not live in 1961, nor did I live in France, which would have made things simpler. Instead, I lived in Long Island City, and in Long Island City, marrowbones are simply not to be had."[17] Given the class and racial diversity of this subdistrict of Queens and the fact that whites are a demographic minority compared to Asian American and Latinx communities, the racial and classed implications of this statement are difficult to overlook. Powell's tone is decidedly frustrated at having to inhabit this particular space that is, at this moment, characterized by what she imagines it doesn't have. Where offal such as marrowbones might often be characterized as excessive food because it is too closely embodied by the inedible parts of the animal, here marrowbones are presented as quintessentially French. In this context, foodstuff that elsewhere might stigmatize certain diets as aberrant and strange now represents a kind of cultural capital that purportedly does not exist in Long Island City. Part of the subtext of her narrative, then, is a sense of privileged entitlement to live elsewhere, temporally and spatially distant from the crowd that composes immigrant life in an outer borough of New York.

At the same time, part of the anxiety at play in this sense of feeling un-homed might be understood as a profound sense of disorientation. Her lack of ease with living in Long Island City is framed as feeling out of place. Ahmed describes how being in place is often understood as knowing which direction to turn in order to find things. When one is at home, one knows how and where to orient the body. One can walk to the kitchen cabinet and immediately find the jar of preserves. One can go into the community and know which section of the local supermarket houses artichokes, which deli carries a particular brand of pasta, which butcher carries particular cuts of beef (or beef marrow). But Ahmed points out that "what we can see in the first place depends on which way we are facing."[18] If one is always uneasy about the space, if one does not know what objects are within their reach, they become unhomed. To not know which way to turn is to experience a profound lack of ease with one's surroundings. But Powell experiences a dizzying sense of disorientation also because Queens, in her imaginary, is an unmoored space, a space of transit and not a space of dwelling. It is her refusal of this space that causes her to feel off-balance in the space she inhabits, thus preventing it from becoming a dwelling.

Anthropologist Martin Manalansan describes how the borough of Queens is considered a conduit to other spaces, but he adds the important caveat that even though "Queens is the site of two of the city's principal airports, LaGuardia and Kennedy, it is not a mere passageway into a cultural and culinary destination elsewhere."[19] Rather, he suggests, Queens can be an intriguing stopping place, particularly in the context of its culinary diversity. Manalansan's numerous ethnographic accounts of the foodways of Queens, by contrast, are more keenly attuned to its culinary complexity and its possibilities for culinary dwelling. In a pair of essays detailing the complex layering of food, race, and class in Queens, Manalansan describes the role of food in the lives of Queens's erstwhile inhabitants, Asian American immigrants.

But where Manalansan sees possibility in Queens's polyvocal, olfactory, and culinary heterogeneity, Powell runs into obstacles. This Queens—the one inhabited by people of color and home to a significant number of Asian immigrant populations—stymies Powell. A consistent refrain in the memoir is the sheer impossibility of the task she sets before her. For Powell, the frustration of her life comes from feeling that she is not affectively a part of the Queens she inhabits—she lives in what she repeatedly dubs (in part for comic effect) "a crappy Queens apartment," but that gesture of disavowing her surroundings firmly marks that her affective place is in an elsewhere.[20] Powell's whiteness is rendered visible through her unwillingness to imagine how she can cook good French food in this particular immigrant milieu. Her version of public space, then, her rendering of Queens as unlivable, puts this particular Asian American space and everyday life under erasure, not only because it denies the possibility that Queens might have a richly textured food life, but also because there is no room in Powell's narrative to imagine how a culinarily complex Queens might provide sustenance and nourishment in the same way that the culinary life of post–World War II Paris allowed Child to thrive. Of note, then, is an observation that speaks to Powell's temporal and physical dislocation from Child's world. As she comments, "Nineteen-sixty-one was a different country, no doubt about it."[21]

The simultaneous resilience and foolhardiness of preparing French food in Queens can also be understood as a temporal and spatial refusal of the complexity of multiracial Queens after 9/11. Instead of attempting to capture the thickness and the uneven texture of the everyday that surrounds her, she allows her everyday to become a version of the reality TV shows that she stares at disconsolately at night in her tiny apartment.[22] The backdrop of Queens is an interesting and complex ethnoracial space that to many is rendered irrelevant at best and, more likely, invisible. Rather, Powell's willful ignorance of the space around her is transplanted onto the bodies around her. Certainly, if Powell has the culinary desire to cook with marrowbones, the logical conclusion to draw is not that Powell is somehow willfully ignorant but that her surroundings are lacking in some fundamental manner. To want to access arcane culinary knowledge is presented as evidence of Powell's cosmopolitan tastes that transcend the purported provincialism of a city that does not easily yield the culinary oddities (paradoxically here they become a necessity) essential to retooling Powell into a cosmopolitan chef.

With all of its intricacies and difficulties and complex techniques, the cultural capital of French food drives Powell's fascination with Child's life in France, whereas Child's life while working in the Office of Strategic Services in Asia is an afterthought. Powell's desire to master French cuisine via Child is symptomatic of her aspirations to solidify her middle-class white femininity. Certainly the conceit of the blog is that Powell aspires to cook like Julia Child. Mastering Child's repertoire of French cooking is the primary way in which Powell is able to orient her subjectivity away from the clamor of post-9/11 New York and toward an imagined future; it is paradoxically about looking backward to Child's France as much as it is about looking forward and away from multiracial Queens. Furthermore, within the pages of *Julie & Julia*, Ceylon (present-day Sri Lanka), India, and China, where Child spent time before moving to France, merely figure as spaces through which Child passes. By and large the only intrigue these spaces hold for Powell is that they are where Julia and Paul Child began their courtship that culminated in a more than forty-year marriage. Asian spaces, then, are mere transits before reaching an elsewhere (postwar France and French cuisine), despite the fact that Child's work in Ceylon with the South East Asia Command under the supervision of Louis Mountbatten was to secure Anglo-American imperial interests in Southeast Asia and South Asia.[23] At the same time, Child was keenly attuned to the cuisine of South and Southeast Asia. Although Powell strategically emphasizes how Paul Child introduced Julia Child to food via French cuisine, it is worth noting that her love affair with food began during their sojourn in Asia. Although Julia Child did not learn how to cook until moving to France, the Childs frequently ate various types of Asian cuisine such as Indonesian *rijsttafel*, an elaborate, multicourse "curry lunch" meal. Consider the following description: "There are three curries: one meat, usually lamb, one fish, usually shrimp, and one fowl, usually chicken. One first lays down a good bed of rice all over a plate, takes generous helpings of each of the three curries, and then covers this all over with as many condiments as the human imagination can devise: chopped coconut flavored with curry powder, paprika, pepper, cardamom, crumbled bacon, crumbled fried bananas, and chutneys of every hue and flavor. The whole is washed down with much beer. It was Julia who organized these in Kandy."[24]

Although this description borders on what Asian American playwright and author Frank Chin describes as food pornography, this aspect of Child's culinary pedigree is omitted from Powell's narrative in favor of her better-known French recipes.[25] The Asian cuisines that Child paradoxically enjoyed are relegated to the margins of Powell's narrative and her imagination.

The politics of Powell's culinary leanings is thus situated within a matrix of nostalgia for an imagined whiteness constructed around privilege and cultural capital, while being defined against class-based categories such as "poor white trash." The strategic fixation on what is deemed "authentic" simultaneously disavows what a fusion-based approach to cooking might allow.[26] By contrast, Powell's dogged pursuit of Julia Child's 1961 Paris experience singularly focuses on the reproduction of an unalloyed French cuisine that is unencumbered by dalliances with otherness, consonant with a middle-class white femininity that structures its desires against forms of otherness. Powell's quest to re-create a kind of culinary purity harkens to another era, one that is not complicated by the clamor and dissonance of everyday life in a racialized space. Fusion and hybridity are not the goal of Powell's foray into the kitchen. In fact, Queens becomes an impediment to pursuing this goal of making authentic French food. None of the ingredients she needs to prepare *concombres au beurre* or *sole meunière* are at her disposal; instead, her investment in middle-class white femininity leads her to navigate the crowds and spaces of the subway so that she can transform the place of her everyday—a tiny apartment in Queens—to an elsewhere, a nostalgically rendered Paris of the 1960s. In this way, Queens is refused from her everyday and her culinary palate, revealing a marked dis-ease with the space she inhabits.[27]

Within this story of urban malaise and a desire to remove herself from the Brown and Black spaces of her immediate environment, Powell locates Julia Child as an icon of whiteness toward which she is oriented. At the end of the narrative, when Powell has reached the end of her travels, she completes her journey with a pilgrimage to Washington, DC, to visit the Julia Child Kitchen exhibit at the Smithsonian National Museum of American History. Her body thus mimics the direction of her desire. Julia Child's kitchen is what Sara Ahmed describes as a kind of "homing device" that orients Powell toward her projected goal. And yet, even en route to this shrine of sorts, Powell is confounded by the presence of racialized bodies. As she attempts to make her way through the crowds of people, she is viscerally disturbed by the proximity of racialized bodies: "Eric had a friend from DC who'd said that parking around the Mall was no problem. This might have been the case on some other day, but it certainly was not on the occasion of the National Association of Negro Women conference and American Black Family Reunion: there were all these dammed trees everywhere plus the masses and masses and masses of people on the Mall didn't walk any faster than the ones crossing the streets."[28] The crowd literally gets in her way, both in New York and now in Washington, DC.

The tourists who populate the Mall are an impediment in the same way that a gathering of African Americans limits her access to the Smithsonian. The pervasive tone of feeling crowded in by hordes of tourists and Black people is not unlike Powell's frustration with having to cook in a cramped kitchen in a crowded borough. Queens is only a space one goes to because one has been priced out of Manhattan and Brooklyn, and yet when one contrasts this with the kind of thick ethnographic work on Queens that Martin Manalansan and others offer in the edited collection *Gastropolis*, one cannot help but notice the very real refusal to see what lies at Powell's doorstep—a flourishing and complex system of immigrant foodways, polyvocal in its intensity and deeply enmeshed in a layered history of race and class. The proximity of Black and Brown bodies crowds Powell, making apparent how she conceives of the internet and blogging as freeing. There, she can be around a community that makes her feel at home. And there, she is comfortably oriented to her goals, a point I will return to later in this chapter.

Gingerly South Asian

Just as Queens is mapped as a space one escapes because the everyday is considered too much, the everyday in Nani Power's *Ginger and Ganesh: Adventures in Indian Cooking, Culture and Love* is framed as a place from which to escape, not because it is not white enough, but because it is too white and not other enough. Describing herself as "not really American: but hard-wired with South Asian taste buds," Power positions herself as someone who is connected to South Asian tastes, viscerally and virtually.[29] Although her sense of being hardwired suggests a proclivity to prefer South Asian flavors (the preference for South Asian tastes is hardwired into her), the term *wired* has an additional layer of meaning when it brushes up against Asian Americans in particular. Where Asian Americans are often dubbed "wired minorities" because of the multiple ways in which internet spaces interpellate Asian Americans as consumers, Power uses the language of digitized subjectivity to explain her willful and strategic appropriation of South Asian tastes.[30] From the outset the conceit of Power's narrative is fairly simple. She wishes to embark on an adventure to cook "real" Indian food and does so in a perhaps unorthodox way. She places an ad simply titled "Please Teach Me Indian Vegetarian Cooking!" in the Northern Virginia section of Craigslist under the Services section. The two-line description characteristic of Craigslist postings notes: "I will bring ingredients and pay you $10/hour for your trouble. I would like to know about your culture as well."[31]

Power immediately sets up a racialized framework for consumption in which an online space like Craigslist allows her to transcend the limitations of geography and networks of intimacy to foment a connection with virtual strangers. Power's book is described as "a yearlong saga of love and spices, found on Craigslist. And what is more modern than that? Years back we had to take an airplane or boat to connect with another culture. These days, we need only have computer access."[32] Here, the internet and access to digital media become the central apparatus that allows Power to build up her culinary arsenal, spinning networks of affiliation that allow her to enter into spaces she might not otherwise be able to access and to establish forms of intimacy with strangers whom she might not ordinarily encounter. Although the book never explicitly discusses how many people respond to Power's ad, nor does it ever really provide their side of the story, it frames this undertaking of looking for food on the internet as being inextricably bound up with the workings of modernity. Global travel and access to vast storehouses of culinary knowledge are on Power's mind, much as they are for Julie Powell. For both writers the tonic or salve against the mundaneness of the everyday requires harnessing the potential of the internet to inhabit alternate geographical spaces and to look beyond the immediate surroundings of each writer's quotidian existence. Unlike Michel de Certeau's claim about the potential of understanding complexity in the everyday, Powell and Power construct the purported banalities of the everyday as limitations. Cooking becomes an escape from the everyday and from the now, propelling one into the realm of the desirable other; in the process, the dangerous stranger becomes domesticated and contained as the intimate ally.

For Power, her desire to find the exotic in the everyday is not hidden. She is an active practitioner of Orientalism but prefers using other terms to describe her particular orientation toward Indian food. She writes: "I am a new growing species in these states—a Disenchanted, Educated, Single, Boomer, Yearning. Indians call themselves *Desis* . . . so I call women like me DESBYS—Wanna-Be Desis. We crave the pageantry, tradition, history, connection, and spirituality of India, yet with our independent, willful, overeducated backgrounds, we would no doubt explode if seriously involved in such a duty-oriented society."[33]

The ease with which she adopts the moniker DESBY, clearly a riff on the more politicized term *Desi*, signals to an inability, or refusal, to engage with the political freight of such a term.[34] To be a wannabe is constructed as positive, for it purportedly speaks to her desire to identify with brownness. Yet she can choose which aspects of Indianness to adopt—namely, the pageantry, spirituality, and so forth; she is too willful to accept the notion of duty. Though inherently problematic for bolstering the Orientalist notion of the duty-bound Indian in opposition to the more defiant Western woman, even more intriguing is the choice of the word *willful*. In this context, to be willful is to recognize the deliberate act of overlooking social inequities.

Following in the vein of Charles Mills's pathbreaking work on ignorance and racism, philosopher Gaile Pohlhaus Jr. probes the nature—and consequences—of particularized forms of ignorance. When ignorance is tied to a refusal to understand the complexity of race—notably, when it is a willful disengagement with the political implications of adopting a latently racist posture—the structuring of this form of thought decidedly becomes an act of willful ignorance. Rather than an individuated act of not knowing, this kind of ignorance is systemically pernicious. Pohlhaus notes that this form of willful hermeneutic ignorance is more than an "act of not 'seeing' parts of the world." It is a "systematic and coordinated misunderstanding of the world."[35] That Power dubs her behavior "childlike" and refers to opting to try on Indianness as her penchant for "play[ing] the role of an Indian" are symptomatic of a willful ignorance of the complex and sullied racial histories behind the notion of "playing Indian."[36] That this strategy of what we might consider willful appropriation is also dubbed "childlike" merely furthers the infantilization of difference. To want to be Indian, or to eat like an Indian, is to be childlike. And yet to want to selectively opt out of certain preconceived notions of Indian womanhood in a particular twist on adopting Brown face is also an act of profound willful ignorance with a history of racism.

Much of the conceit of this book is premised on the notion of ignorance, and this fact is not insignificant. From the first beat, Power announces her project as being embedded within a matrix of not knowing. Not knowing is simultaneously about claiming ignorance and about considering any attempt to counter ignorance as necessarily positive. To want to know more about what is epistemologically unavailable to her is seen as positive, yet little negotiation occurs around what makes her particularized claims to ignorance notably Orientalist. What she wants can be easily transacted via Craigslist, but her desires are also about orienting herself toward certain forms of knowledge and, by implication, away from others.

That Power turns to Craigslist to abet her ignorance is complicated, and complex, in numerous ways. Although her year of cooking Indian food took place before the infamous case of Philip Markoff, the erstwhile Craigslist Killer, the desire to turn to a space both celebrated and maligned for providing the pleasures and dangers of anonymous encounters has a decidedly manic quality. In some ways it can be considered a space that subverts the machinations of commodity capitalism, constructing a decentered capitalism, but

Craigslist has also become a place to find things or liaisons outside of one's everyday sphere of activity, seemingly endorsing the notion that anything and everything, including people, is for sale or easily obtained. Whether through having anonymous sexual encounters, selling furniture, or trading cooking lessons, Craigslist functions as a virtual space that can potentially reconfigure and create new geographic intimacies that do not necessarily follow traditional mappings and lines of community.[37] Although Power uses Craigslist (albeit not to procure sex or to find a date), she remains orientated toward particular forms of knowledge and acquisition; nevertheless, she very clearly turns to Craigslist with the idea that anything is for sale, including the labor of women of color. Here it is the allure of the other, whom she suspects is in suburbia but is not visible to her, that she seeks out. There is something intriguingly illicit about the kind of desire she seeks to legitimize—to consume the other, to exoticize the other whom she imagines hiding in plain sight—and at the same time it feeds into the machinations of this decentered commodity capitalism.[38]

Of particular note is the concerted effort to blur the line between stranger and friend (or intimate ally) that undergirds the dialogic move in Power's move to locate Indian American women who turn to the internet to find community. As Sara Ahmed has argued, the ontological position of the stranger demarcates social space. One is a stranger because they are deemed not to belong; at the same time, the multicultural stranger—the immigrant woman in suburban Washington, DC—is also always already an outsider because of her status as an outsider who can be assimilated into the heterogeneous "we" of the nation and "well-meaning white subjects."[39]

In the chapter titled "Vishnu of Suburbia" (and the book is full of titles that rely on a knee-jerk Orientalism, ostensibly aimed to evoke humor, such as "Spices with Benefits" and "Spice Spice Baby"), she is surprised that the suburbs, home to a large number of Indian Americans, would also be populated with Indian bodies. Her vision of where Indians make homes, where they dwell, adheres to a notion of the suburbs that Lynn Spigel describes as imagining bodies of color as out of place in the suburbs. But whereas Spigel is rightfully aware of how this notion of the suburb is limited by its refusal to engage the complex realities of which spaces are homes to nonnormative bodies, Power can conjure only surprise when she drives through suburban Asian America and sees "strangers" making homes in these places.[40] Recent ethnographic work on suburbanization and Asian Americans reveals the suburbs to be heterotopic spaces of racial and ethnic difference, counter to what Power imagines. Notably, S. Mitra Kalita's and Karen Tongson's respective studies of suburban New Jersey and Southern California reveal the suburbs to be more complex spaces of dwelling than heretofore conceived: not only are suburbs home to immigrant and queer communities, but their growth and expansion are direct consequences of altering patterns of global migration and settlement that have resulted in strangers making homes in the US.[41] As Tongson notes, the Hollywood suburban filmic aesthetic of "a dark underbelly of psychic dysfunction" is in stark contrast to what contemporary configurations of suburban Asian American space actually look like.[42] The spaces that are thickly populated by Indian immigrants, such as the places to which Power travels to find authentic Indian home cooking, are complex forms of urban settlement. According to geographer Wei Li, the ethnoburb has been forged from the interplay of economic globalization, political struggle between and within nation-states, major US immigration policy shifts, and a host of local conditions. The ethnoburb cannot simply represent an attempt to assimilate, but must be understood as a space where different kinds of subjectivities can emerge.[43]

Power's foray into suburbs and apartment complexes—spaces that are home to large communities of Indian immigrants, as Kalita points out—is enabled by her strategic use of social media (Craigslist) to orient herself toward communities and strangers who are largely invisible to her. For Power, seeking out Brown bodies is central to the act of pushing her narrative forward, whereas when confronted with strange communities of Brown bodies, Powell can only articulate frustration. But central to that quest—and not unlike the quest described in *Eat, Pray, Love*—is the idea that cooking is about a kind of self-indulgent form of personal fulfillment more than an ethical form of self-care. For Power, Craigslist provides a way to orient herself toward her desires. The construction of this dichotomy between the self and the other, where the self is unmistakably the "modern American woman, the DESBY, if you will," and the culinary as evidenced by the popularity of Martha Stewart, the Food Network, cooking classes, and so on, prompts Power to claim that American women "need to reclaim this territory [of the kitchen] again, on our own terms."[44] Of particular note is the fact that Power acknowledges Asian American bodies and labor in a way that Powell refuses to or is unable to see. Yet even though Power's text orients itself toward rendering visible the spaces and narratives of South Asian American culinary complexity, its focus on understanding difference as a fetish remains complicit in creating an erasure of the history and systemic absence, or at minimum, an elision, of the Asian American subject and the spaces of Asian American dwelling. Asian American homes are spaces Power visits, but her foray is necessarily limited because no moment of a kind of radical synthesis or fusion exists wherein Power's narrative gives pause to the particular forms of settlement that have turned suburbs of Northern Virginia into more than mere spaces inhabited by "strange" Brown bodies, but vibrant spaces of dwelling occasioned by changing patterns in globalization and economic forces. Instead, these spaces of settlement are places to visit via a form of culinary tourism, whereby to consume the knowledge and histories of subjects marked as "other" becomes self-empowering in the most self-indulgent form imaginable.

Neoliberal Multiculturalism and the White Culinary Imaginary

Remarkably, both texts create narratives about escaping the mundane or everyday by seeking refuge in alterity, or perhaps in sameness, doing so through their engagement with food. And yet, these two works, notable for their desire to better the self through an escape from the everyday, are part of a larger subgenre of writing that is constructed on a narrative about a typically yearlong foray into a different world. One of the most well-known exemplars of this genre is Elizabeth Gilbert's *Eat, Pray, Love* (2007). For Gilbert, the conceit is to write about traveling to three countries in order to understand food, spirituality, and love in her life. Similarly, Barbara Kingsolver's *Animal, Vegetable, Miracle* (2008) chronicles a year in the life of the author's (and her family's) commitment to eating locally. Katherine Russell Rich's *Dreaming in Hindi: Coming Awake in Another Language* (2009), *The Happiness Project* by Gretchen Rubin (2009), and *Orange Is the New Black* by Piper Kerman (2011) are also a part of this trend, which Ruth Williams describes as producing a new kind of "female neoliberal spiritual subject" invested in a form of self-discovery that occurs not through critical reflection on the self and society, but with "spiritual" consumption.[45] Further, the publication of these texts or the release of cinematic versions often coincide with each other or occur within relatively short succession. *Ginger and Ganesh*, for example, was released at the same time that *Eat Pray Love* was hitting screens. Remarkably, both texts stage the journey of a disaffected middle-class white woman who seeks to find personal fulfillment and enrichment through a strategic Orientalizing of the other. With much celebratory rhetoric noting how the film's protagonist, the recently divorced Elizabeth Gilbert, overcame harsh odds in her unrelenting pursuit of happiness, the film was an instant success. Her happiness was to be found in Italy, India, and Indonesia, in the worlds outside of her quotidian existence. Based on the author's travels over the course of a year, *Eat, Pray, Love*, first a memoir then a film, takes its readers (or viewers) through what has been described as the ultimate form of self-indulgent travel. Gilbert self-consciously travels only to countries beginning with the letter "I"—Italy, India, and Indonesia—along the way constructing a narrative of self-discovery. In Italy, Gilbert eats; India is the space where she turns inward, accessing her spiritual self; and on the island of Bali, Gilbert finds love. Per Arjun Appadurai's now-classic formulation about modernity's phases of capitalism, the imagination is "central to all forms of agency, is itself a social fact, and is the key component of the new global order; these landscapes are eventually navigated by agents who both experience and constitute larger formations, in part from their own sense of what these landscapes offer."[46] For Elizabeth Gilbert, the landscapes of each space she travels through offer a singular experience and a mode of understanding an aspect of herself.

The other as constructed by *Eat, Pray, Love* thus emerges as a foundation upon which to build the architecture of one's life, revealing the asymmetrical positions assigned to women of color and the global White traveler. Food becomes important to the goal of promoting possibility for one kind of subject (the global traveler) while simultaneously limiting the possible scope of agency and complexity for another. When women of color are valued it is because they are able to enrich the lives of the white middle-class American women who stand at the center of narratives like *Eat, Pray, Love* and *Ginger and Ganesh*. Where communities of women of color come from and how are rendered secondary in these narratives, effectively erasing any historical complexity of their everyday lives. To put it in terms of a fictional narrative that was wildly popular in summer 2011, women of color hold maximum value when they are able to function as the help.[47]

Such solipsism may be seen to be part and parcel of this genre of life writing, and certainly the autobiographical impulse in some strands of women's writing decreases its value in traditional patriarchal modes of reading. Moreover, little is arguably new about Orientalist narratives predicated on ushering out the woman of color in order to yield space for the emergence of the white woman's subjectivity.[48] Certain kinds of narratives position women of color in the position of helping middle-class white women better themselves, thus providing a rich context for understanding why Powell feels irritated that she is unable to find the ingredients for her culinary experiments in Queens.

This genre of writing implicitly suggests that the story of a woman of color is to be valued only if it tells us something about the journey of the middle-class white woman and why, in the case of Power, a move can be made that entitles one to claim the identity of a "DESBY." But rather than dismiss memoir as an exploration of the self, it is important to consider who must bear the burdens of this genre of self-exploration and under what circumstances such labor occurs. A different range of possibilities for forming communities, predicated on mutuality, emerges when the primary goal of the writer's quest is to productively problematize power dynamics in lieu of creating a narrative oriented toward self-improvement that effectively reasserts the hegemonic place of white womanhood.

Throughout this chapter, I have been gesturing to Heidegger's notion of dwelling and Sara Ahmed's notion of orienting bodies toward objects and others as a means of working through the relationships to power and knowledge fostered by Powell and Power. Central to my analysis has been a negotiation around the notion of lived spaces. In particular, when one reconceptualizes what constitutes home and lived spaces, one is more able to explore how the feeling of being unhomed in particular sites might foment new kinds of dwelling. Heidegger suggests that to dwell in a place is not the same as to inhabit a space.[49] The culinary functions in both texts as the occasion to allow the subject (in this case the middle-class white woman) to work through the notion of inhabiting a place while being oriented toward dwelling in a different sociotemporal geography. With this radical asymmetry between what it means to inhabit a particular location (multiracial Queens for Powell and bland whiteness for Power) and to look to find a place of dwelling, a place of living where one can orient one's body and desires toward and against Asian American and immigrant spaces, be they in the crowded thickness of Queens or the texture of suburban Northern Virginia, Power suggests that her quest for personal fulfillment and betterment is about finding a way back to the kitchen. But in Power's case, to inhabit the kitchen, to transform it into a space of dwelling, requires the labor of others.

One cannot, of course, overlook the fact that both Power and Powell describe feelings of being unhomed. It is notable that Powell's narrative becomes aligned with the similar kinds of erasures of history and race that post-9/11 discourses about tragedy produced, wherein Brown and poor bodies remained unseen and outside of the structures of public mourning, insofar that Powell also does not see the historical-racial complexity of the neighborhood at her doorstep. For Powell, much of her year of living in Queens and cooking her way through Julia Child's tome is about orienting herself and her desires to other spaces and other possibilities. For the yearlong period of the experiment, her blog provided a space to dwell, both intellectually and affectively. As she notes in an interview, "The project became like the spine of my life, and everything else was built around it."[50] Her affective here could be the blog, a space she could occupy in a virtual space, build community, and think. The blog provided more than a virtual escape from her surroundings. To write about each recipe and to include personal narratives, the kinds which are permissible, even desirable, in food blogging, was to create a new space of dwelling and possibility that in some small measure seemed to make it possible, however problematically, to sever the connection between where one lives and where one dwells. Although Power uses Craigslist as a way to access spaces hidden from her (or so she imagines) more than as a place to build community, one cannot overlook the power of the digital virtual environment for her project either. Like Powell's blog, Power's Craigslist advertisement, evidenced by its reproduction at the beginning of the narrative, is the spine of Power's life; without it, there could be no place from which to build a narrative. Moreover, each project offers radically different interpretations of the internet as racialized space.

As I have been arguing, the tone and tenor of Powell's narrative suggest that she turns to her blog to create a kind of community that is free of the clamor and dissonance of post-9/11 New York. Turning to Child is at once a retreat to comfort food and a retreat into whiteness. Yet Powell does this at a time when the internet, and particularly the blogosphere, is transforming from a space of whiteness to a space where young women of color thrive; as I noted earlier, they are among the population who uses social media networking platforms the most. In notable contrast, Power's turn to Craigslist is precisely about seeking out color in her life, reducing multiculturalism into a form of fetishized consumer culture. Each text implicitly racializes its imagined and desired audience in ways that are simultaneously consonant with and divergent from statistics about the racial, gendered, and classed demographic makeup of the typical user of social media platforms such as Craigslist and the blogosphere. A 2012 issue of *New Formations* focusing on the topic of food and race aimed to provide thick engagement with palatable multiculturalisms and the politics of turning to the other or the figure of the stranger in order to consume difference. In his introduction to the issue, Ben Highmore describes "a troubled cosmopolitanism: one that wants to promote convivial cultural mingling . . . but one that knows too well that racism and inter-cultural anxiety has found a long-standing foothold in the negotiation of food."[51] "Troubled cosmopolitanism" describes the tensions that undergird each of these texts. For these undoubtedly educated, young, willful feminists, negotiations with food provide occasions for imagining the kinds of worlds produced by their respective texts.

Visceral discomfort with who and where they are becomes the driving force behind their search to dwell in an elsewhere, not here or now. They are most certainly troubled by the terms of their cosmopolitanism, not being in place in their bodies or their socio-temporal location makes their homes giddy spaces. In the end it is precisely this feeling of giddiness—an unease with being too white, an unease with not being white enough—that orients Power and Powell to want to inhabit other spaces.

Coda

In the epigraph to this chapter I quote a short section from Lawrence Dai's blog, *The Lawrence/Julie and Julia Project* (2011). Dai's blog is a meta-reflection on the film version of *Julie & Julia*. During his yearlong experiment, Dai, an Asian American student at Northwestern University, proposes to watch the film every day and to blog about a different aspect of the film. Although he composes the blog entries with humor in mind, one entry in particular is worth discussing in more detail. On day 116 of his experiment, March 25, 2011, Dai visits Tu Lan, a Vietnamese eatery in San Francisco. Noted on several social media sites as a place where Julia Child was reputed to have enjoyed many meals, Tu Lan overtly showcases this information on its menu, and not surprisingly, Julia Child's iconic claim to fame buttresses Tu Lan's own claim to fame. The front of the takeout menu prominently displays a sketch of Julia Child, and Lawrence Dai's blog shows him pictured next to a framed copy of the menu.

In the photograph a markedly non–French chef version of Julia Child is enjoying a bowl of steaming *pho*. Dai's photograph of him posing with the menu and pointing at the object orients him to the menu. The juxtaposition of this smiling Asian American man pointing to culinary icon Julia Child interrupts the purported whiteness of Julia Child. Here is the domestic grande dame of French cuisine serving as an icon for a dish that is arguably the signature culinary item for one of France's most long-standing colonies, Vietnam. That it is Vietnamese food Child is depicted eating is most intriguing in terms of establishing a larger continuum between colonial and postcolonial cuisine. Intentionality notwithstanding, Dai's blog entry on Julia Child's fondness for Tu Lan gestures toward the possibility of understanding the parameters of "French" cuisine in a much more expansive sense. Although the popular website Yelp describes Tu Lan as straddling several neighborhoods including the racially mixed and queer Tenderloin District and the governmental complex of Civic Center, urban geographer Damon Scott suggests that the location of Tu Lan is much more complex than Yelp might suggest:

> [Tu Lan] is on a several block strip of low-rent (un-gentrified) buildings on Sixth Street that sticks out like a panhandle across Market Street. The core of the Tenderloin is on the northside of Market (bounded by Market, Larkin, Geary, and Mason). The Tenderloin corresponds roughly to a police precinct that functioned as an "anything goes" holding area for business activities/people/land uses that were excluded from other areas. The term tenderloin is reputedly from the expensive cut of meat the cops got in this district because of the bribes and kickbacks they got for allow[ing] brothels, speakeasies, prostitution, queer bars, rooming houses for trans people/drag performers . . . . More recently the Tenderloin has become the place of arrival for Southeast Asian immigrants (particularly Vietnamese) who have developed a visible, semi-official commercial district along Larkin Street—the western boundary of the Tenderloin . . . [(]called "Little Saigon"). There are intense redevelopment pressures on the "Mid-Market Area"—a planner's construct for the "unimproved" area between the Civic Center and Powell subway/BART stations. The Union Square/Powell Street area to [the] east is the heart of the city's convention/hotel/tourism/shopping economy. Civic Center on the west is the government complex (that includes some new federal buildings, and is growing). The Tenderloin is the area being squeezed in the middle. Labeling Tu Lan a "Civic Center" restaurant makes it sound like it's in a better neighborhood than it is . . . and is perhaps aspirational on the part of planners.[52]

Scott's observations suggest that Tu Lan's location places it at the heart of a racially diverse and queer neighborhood. And during my many visits to Tu Lan, I have noticed the way in which the increasingly gentrified sections of Market Street adjacent to the location of Tu Lan encroach upon the space of the dwindling population of homeless and itinerant people in the area. As such it has strains of commonality with Powell's Queens in terms of being home to marginalized subjects. Yet the fact that one comes to remark on Child's penchant for no-frills Vietnamese food via Lawrence Dai's blog, instead of any of the multiple iterations of Julie Powell's narratives about Julia, is telling. Just as Julie remains oriented to Child's whiteness (looking away from Queens toward 1950s France), she also misses vital elements of Child's interest in non-Western food.

I mention Dai's blog here because it foregrounds similar conclusions about the whiteness of *Julie & Julia* that I gesture toward, while also signaling a way to rupture that narrative. In the description of his blog Dai notes, "I hope to learn as much, if not more, [than Julie Powell] by watching the film *Julie & Julia* every day for a year."[53] Although humor, often of the scatological variety, guides much of the blog, it remains keenly attuned to recognizing the limitations of where Powell's narrative wants to go or can go. Noting that he wishes to learn more than, and not simply as much as, Julie Powell speaks to a recognition of where Powell's project is limited.[54] What is more, the blog is titled *The Lawrence/Julie and Julia Project*. Grammatically, I suggest, the use of a slash rather than the word *and* suggests a rupture in the film. Lawrence of the blog interrupts the blog, forming his own readings of and relationship to the figure of Julia, presenting a form of what Lisa Nakamura calls "digital racial formation." The slash is also reminiscent of David Palumbo-Liu's articulation of "Asian/American," which does away with the hyphen and the space that are arguably more common and which literary critic David L. Eng and others have critiqued.[55] For Palumbo-Liu the slash is a grammatical sign that militates against the deferral of Asian to American. The slash facilitates understanding the liaisons between "Asian" and "American." It "at once instantiates a choice between two terms, their simultaneous and equal status, and an element of undecidability, that is, as it at once implies both exclusion and inclusion."[56]

Dai's blog demands that a similar choice be made between Lawrence and Julie—neither identity is stable, nor is the relationship with Julia stable. The slash between Lawrence's name and Julie's name is both unsettling and inclusive. It points out that Julie's narrative is incomplete, partial, fragmentary. But the term on the other side of the dyad—or in this case, triad—is also unstable. Refusing a binary identity also refuses the simple dualities that undergird Powell's text. Dai's blog seems to suggest that a conversation between two white women, inaugurated on the internet, is not only problematic but also untenable. And in the end, Dai's blog, however playful it might seem, also puts forward a radically different idea of an intimate eating public. Predicated on the notion that people of color are also participants in conversations about food on the internet, Dai's blog is perhaps one way to imagine an alternate mode of dwelling, one always in flux but always oriented toward redefining what meanings accrue around the representation of culinary practices and the kinds of eating publics they produce.

In his review of the 2014 indie film *Chef*, *New York Times* film reviewer Stephen Holden summarizes the film thus: "Food trucks, Twitter wars and salsa music: *Chef* has its pinkie on the pulse of the moment."[1] A film that narrates the fall and rise of Los Angeles–based and Miami-born chef Carl Casper (played by Jon Favreau), *Chef* is one of the first feature films to prominently feature the food truck in its narrative trajectory. When Casper finds working as a chef in a typical brick-and-mortar restaurant to be uninspiring because it does not afford him the option to be as culinarily creative as he would hope, he finds himself at the receiving end of a food critic's negative comments on Twitter. His food, the film critic in the movie suggests, lacks flavor because the chef lacks the passion to make good food. An ensuing battle over social media results in Casper losing his job. But in keeping with this film genre, where hard work can triumph over adversity, Casper eventually finds his way back into the kitchen and is convinced to travel to Miami. While in Miami he reconnects with his love of food in a way that he was unable to amid the noise of Los Angeles.

As the film progresses Casper's culinary passion begins to take shape. He enlists the help of his young son, Percy, and his friend Martin, and together they restore a decrepit food truck and begin to serve *Cubanos*, the signature sandwich of Miami. He begins selling his food in Miami and embarks on a cross-country trip in the newly refurbished food truck. On the road to Los Angeles, Percy, a social media aficionado, promotes the food truck on platforms such as Twitter and Facebook, and the food truck becomes a popular and critical sensation among diners across the country, who line up to sample Casper's

Cubanos. By the end of the film, Casper's venture has become a financial and critical success. He has found a way to mesh his creative passion for cooking with a successful model of entrepreneurship that successfully harnesses the power of social media. Through social media Casper is able to create a new type of eating public, one which draws strangers to him in every city because of their love for food. Ultimately, whereas the brick-and-mortar restaurant did not allow him the creativity to cook his kind of food, the business model of the food truck allowed him to become the kind of chef he always wanted to be. He becomes more deeply connected with his customers, even as he moves from city to city, and he is able to create and serve the kind of food that makes him happy. Although these intimacies are temporary at best, they also endure in the sense that the provisional eating publics created in each city are documented on social media. By the time the food truck is ready to move to the next city, an eating public has already formed, eagerly awaiting the arrival of Casper's food truck and his signature sandwiches. Toward the end of the film Casper returns home and reintegrates into the culinary scene of Los Angeles, reclaiming his place as a favorite son among LA foodies.

In the early part of the twenty-first century, food trucks were a vital and emerging part of the food scene of any major city. Part of a city's claim to a robust foodie culture was the presence of a varied and consistent food truck scene. At the peak of the food truck boom, the Food Network capitalized on the burgeoning interest in food truck culture with its reality-based cooking competition show *The Great Food Truck Race*. Similarly, the Cooking Channel describes "food cart fare [as] the hottest trend going" and its show *Eat St.* as a "lip-smacking celebration of North America's tastiest, messiest and most irresistible street food . . . your grease-stained roadmap to the ultimate street food experience."[2] Although contemporary food culture may have considered the food truck to be a fad, the food truck itself has a long history, particularly in working-class communities in cities like Los Angeles, where the humble lunch cart, known as the *lonchera*, caters to the primarily working-class Mexican clientele outside of main thoroughfares and popular hotspots. Food writer Gustavo Arellano describes newer food trucks as "luxe loncheras" but also makes a point of noting their indebtedness to and difference from the more humble lonchera. Arellano notes, "America didn't embrace the food truck, long the domain of the working-class and—here in Southern California—Mexicans[,] until Kogi and hipsters made them the fad that they are today. If it wasn't for the years of legal fights these *loncheras*[3] engaged in—without Twitter, Facebook or much start-up cash—you wouldn't have these big festivals, or young chefs dreaming of amazing fusions within the confines of moveable metal."[4] Arellano rightly points out that although the food truck might have emerged as a favorite among an emergent class of upwardly mobile diners always eager to access culinary innovation, the food truck itself has a far less glamorous history. The food truck, or lonchera, gained traction in cities like Los Angeles by serving humble, everyday food to working-class Mexican Americans who were in need of cheap meals to eat on the go while working. Whereas day laborers would often be refused service or made to feel unwelcome at conventional restaurants, the traditional lonchera welcomed them and provided easy and inexpensive access to food.

The luxe lonchera, on the other hand, began to emerge as a symbol of leisurely eating at the onset of the millennium. Food trucks typically have catchy names like Curry Up Now, Easy Slider, Guac n' Roll, and Nacho Bizness, and they often gain traction by relying on a particular gimmick to draw customers in.[5] In effect the food truck had successfully extricated itself from its working-class origins.

Although the height of interest in food trucks may have passed, it remains worthwhile to revisit this moment from the recent past and to account for the emergence of the luxe lonchera as a novelty, when in reality food trucks have long been a fixture in, and necessity for, working-class communities that do not fit the bourgeois and neoliberal multicultural ideas of who can access the sit-down restaurant. In particular, the nouveau food truck sells not just food but an aspirational lifestyle that distinguishes it from the lonchera. More than simply serving up food that caters to a markedly different clientele than do traditional loncheras, these new forms of mobile dining also appeal to different aesthetic and political sensibilities. Eating from a food truck becomes about accessing something new and different, and the kinds of foods they serve are in marked contradistinction to the foods served by more traditional food trucks. The earlier forms of mobile dining catered specifically to working-class individuals who would feel out of place at a sit-down restaurant because of their embodiment (their race, the physical and sensory traces of manual labor—dirt, sweat—and their class status). Earlier food trucks also made it possible for people with short lunch breaks (construction workers, day laborers, etc.) to grab quickly a calorie-dense meal without spending a lot of time waiting for or eating a meal. They had (and continue to have) a specific function that has little to do with lingering over a meal. They are a vital piece in the larger picture that makes up the world of the eating public—but one that is driven by the needs of the laboring, rather than consuming, classes.

In distinction to the traditional food truck is the luxe lonchera, which seeks to actively exclude this group of laborers from their clientele in favor of younger diners, the hip urban foodies always in search of a new adventure. And yet one of the benefits of the luxe lonchera is that it allows chefs who might not otherwise have access to the capital to build and develop a brick-and-mortar restaurant to build a public presence and create a base of loyal followers. In this narrative the telos is not unlike that which is mapped by the film *Chef*. The initial impetus to open a food truck may come from a lack of access to funding and a need to be flexible, but the ultimate goal, as the film *Chef* suggests, is to open a brick-and-mortar restaurant. In this context we can better understand why, for a brief time after the 2008 economic recession, luxe loncheras started popping up all over the United States. Central to the appeal of the luxe lonchera is that it fully embraces the model of mobile dining. Loyal clients remain apprised about the location of the food truck through social media. As food writer Jonathan Gold notes:

> The thrill of Kogi, Nom Nom, Grill Em All, Glowfish and the other new trucks lay in their mobility, their ever-shifting set of possibility. Very few of the loncheras, by contrast, ever moved at all. There was an entire taxonomy of loncheras as rooted to their spots as any brick-and-mortar cafe: tethered trucks that often attract immense crowds on weekends while their mothership restaurants 25 feet away, with identical menus, lie empty; the cemitas wagons, serving Puebla-style hoagies stuffed with thin, pounded fried beef, avocado, hand-shredded quesillo and smoky chipotle chiles; tamaleros vending banana-leaf-wrapped Salvadoran tamales as well as champurrado, a warm, delicious beverage of spiced chocolate thickened with masa; or even the fruit carts, identifiable by their gaily colored umbrellas, which prepare cocktails of pineapple, mango, papaya, grapes and watermelon, seasoned with powdered chile, salt and a squeeze of lime.[6]

As an ambivalent enthusiast of the food truck scene, I am always curious to see how each food truck curates the culinary and simultaneously functions as a purveyor of food and as a performative object. I initially became interested in food trucks when they started emerging in cities like Los Angeles. My first visit to a food truck was during a meeting of the Modern Language Association in Los Angeles in 2010. Like many others, I had heard of Roy Choi, his food truck called Kogi, and his "Korean tacos," but I had never had one, and I was wary that it was just a culinary gimmick. I learned through Twitter that Choi would be setting up shop during the lunch hour at a location not far from the conference venue in downtown Los Angeles. I arranged to go with a couple of friends, and we decided we would sample as many different items on the menu as possible. I was not disappointed when I savored the taste of Choi's fabled short rib taco and kimchi quesadilla. Even for a seasoned foodie like me, this Korean Mexican fusion was a relatively new taste at the time, and it signaled to a new kind of cuisine that young Asian Americans were creating. Throughout the intervening years, Kogi and its proprietor Roy Choi became widely recognized as a doyen of this new kind of cuisine. Whereas fusion cuisine had dominated the culinary landscape of the early 2000s, Choi was doing something different with Kogi. He was not showcasing assimilable foods, blending the tastes of Asian food with those of recognizable Western fare; rather, at Kogi Choi was combining two minor cuisines—Korean and Mexican— to create a different kind of fusion cuisine. Cognizant of their cultural capital within the contemporary urban foodie market, food truck owners have the potential to wield significant cultural power in shaping taste mechanisms while providing innovative takes on cuisines, often in combinations that are deemed new or unusual—the phenomenon of the Korean taco a case in point.[7]

At the same time, the food truck cannot be wrested from its location within larger sociopolitical forces. As Ernesto Hernandez-Lopez notes, loncheras do not always meet with celebratory zeal by policymakers and city officials invested in gentrification. Under the guise of "quality of life" campaigns, in a 2008 taco truck war such political actors took aim at loncheras, describing them as "a cumbersome and unsightly form of vending."[8] In addition, antivendor perspectives (which include those of large commercial restaurants) target loncheras, arguing that "food trucks congest streets and sidewalks" and deeming loncheras in public areas to be "unsafe and unsanitary."[9] The newer food trucks or luxe loncheras represent a form of cultural innovation and foodie culture, whereas the traditional loncheras are subject to racialized discourses that construct them as foreign, undesirable, and unsanitary. Luxe loncheras, then, have to find particular niche markets to demonstrate how they are at the cutting edge of innovative new cuisine. By offering a new take on the taco or the *dosa*, food trucks of the luxe lonchera variety do more than "serve" food. They also actively produce an image of urban cool and hipness: edible art for the palate in no small measure.

The food truck or the luxe lonchera has been successful because it rids the working-class cuisine of its scent of otherness. As George Orwell noted in *The Road to Wigan Pier*, a quasi-ethnographic work about poor mining communities in Northern England, one of the defining ways in which class distinctions operated was through smell. Noting the ways he as a self-described member of the upper middle class was taught to look down on the poor, he writes:

> Here you come to the real secret of class distinctions in the West—the real reason why a European of bourgeois upbringing, even when he calls himself a Communist, cannot without a hard effort think of a working man as his equal. It is summed up in four frightful words which people nowadays are chary of uttering, but which were bandied about quite freely in my childhood. The words were: *The lower classes smell.* That was what we were taught—the lower classes smell. And here, obviously, you are at an impassable barrier. For no feeling of like or dislike is quite so fundamental as a physical feeling. . . . However well you may wish him, however much you may admire his mind and character, if his breath stinks he is horrible and in your heart of hearts you will hate him. It may not greatly matter if the average middle-class person is brought up to believe that the working classes are ignorant, lazy, drunken, boorish, and dishonest; it is when he is brought up to believe that they are dirty that the harm is done. And in my childhood we were brought up to believe that they were dirty.[10]

Orwell's assessment seizes on an important point about how class distinction and difference works. The scent, or stench, of otherness—whether real or imagined—stigmatizes working-class bodies of color. The luxe lonchera, aware of this "stench of otherness," has carefully worked to rehabilitate the image of the food truck and to create a more sanitized and palatable version of alterity. In this context the refusal of certain people to patronize Mexican food trucks—uncharitably known as "roach coaches" because they fail to signify as food trucks per se in this new culinary landscape—is no mere accident. Rather, this deliberate repackaging of difference signals how cuisines must be made over and sanitized in order to sell food outside of their communities of origin. Certain cuisines are tainted with the scent or odor of otherness and seemingly interrupt the culinary experience for the neoliberal multicultural subject. Two distinct kinds of eating publics emerge: those who patronize loncheras to access quick, cheap, and filling fare, and those who seek a novel culinary experience via the luxe lonchera. These two publics do not overlap but are deliberately kept distinct from one another. The luxe lonchera, then, it might be said, carries a particular cultural cachet because of its ability to sell a lifestyle or idea. It is never only food that is on the menu, but also a certain kind of mediated experience of sociality designed to broker intimacies among avowed foodies.

I begin with this journey through the uneven landscape of the food truck, the lonchera, and the luxe lonchera as a way to enter into a larger conversation about the cultural work that the food truck can perform in a moment that is purportedly postracial and insistently embraces the global. It is certainly true that the food truck is of a certain social moment (in 2022 it may seem passé); nonetheless, it allows us to inquire into the ways that these particular culinary spaces advance conversations about how eating in public is rarely only about the food itself. Instead, these forms of mobile dining also rely on creating a form of sociality that allows consumers to imagine different ways of coming together around food. It is no coincidence that the most successful food trucks often are those that repackage familiar and comfortable foods via a gimmick of sorts. Whether a Korean taco or a fancified grilled cheese sandwich or hamburger, one does not have to stray far from one's comfort zone when buying food from a luxe lonchera. The cultural capital that accrues behind the luxe lonchera often allows it to make a range of culinary styles readily accessible, suggesting that we live and eat in a globalized world that is also deemed to be postracial.

But what happens when the food truck aims to provide a different kind of experience with culinary sociality? What if the point of eating is not merely to taste something new but to think anew about food and its provenance, to make diners question the terms by which food is imagined to be globally available? What if the goal of the food truck is to ask consumers not simply to eat with their taste buds but also to consider how a particular culinary novelty found its way onto their plate? In this way, what happens when purveyors of food, notably performance artists, harness the history of mobile eating to engage more deeply questions of culinary sociality that would lead them to think about how certain kinds of intimate eating publics emerge?

The food truck as performative object owes much to artistic movements like Fluxus: artists utilize food-as-art installation as an occasion to foster social and political commentary and thereby initiate conversations about the circulation and consumption of food. Among the better-known exemplars within radical food art practices are Alison Knowles's work and performance with the Fluxus group in the 1960s. For Knowles, the simple act of making a salad (comprising edible ingredients) in a public space and then inviting the public to collectively eat the prepared dish functions to establish the link among art, eating, and community.[11]

The interactive nature of food in these venues stresses the importance of thinking about food as shared practice in which the audience member's participation is a necessary element of the aesthetic experience of the art installation. As suggested by the Smart Museum of Art in Chicago, "numerous artists have used the simple act of sharing food and drink to advance aesthetic goals and to foster critical engagement with the culture of their moment. These artist-orchestrated meals can offer a radical form of hospitality that punctures everyday experience, using the meal as a means to shift perceptions and spark encounters that aren't always possible in a fast-moving and segmented society."[12]

To press this idea further: What if the experience of eating actively values spaces of discomfort, conflict, and the thorny? When one's palate is sated, what kinds of questions can one ask about the radical asymmetries emerging from a culture of intolerance that structures what is deemed edible and inedible? It is precisely this question about what it means to eat that which is considered inedible—not only because it is too foreign but because it may be tainted by the undesirable immigrant or even by something considered "evil" or from the realm of the terrorist—that prompts my inquiry in this chapter. Shifting from the focus in the previous chapter, wherein writers create spaces of culinary intimacy with other individuals via foods they fetishize, thereby rendering the stranger into a safe figure, this chapter asks what it means to ingest the food of the "enemy," or a figure who is not so easily recuperated into a framework that would cast some as unwelcome strangers—what I refer to, following the cue of the artists I discuss, as "enemies"—whereas other strangers are safe, palatable, and welcome. When food is prepared by the hands of the so-called enemy, when food actively bears the sign of the enemy and refuses a more palatable moniker, a different kind of intimate eating public emerges. In the world of the luxe lonchera, where fusion is all the rage, unpalatability is kept carefully at bay (unless the particular cultural capital comes from the extreme nature of the cuisine). But what happens when that conflict is not obscured, but brought into radical focus? To examine these questions I turn to two different sites, an art installation titled *Enemy Kitchen*, and Conflict Kitchen, a now-defunct takeout restaurant in Pittsburgh, Pennsylvania, that create different kinds of intimate eating publics, ones in which people—often strangers—come together to share food in provisional spaces for short periods of time.

Notably, the provenance of these "enemy" foods is often countries that have not been enfolded into a vision of US multiculturalism because they are often embroiled in diplomatic controversy or combat with the US. In juxtaposing these sites and exploring the performative politics deployed within each context, I explore what it means to turn to the tactile, olfactory, and consumptive to reflect on questions of US diplomacy and foreign policy that have taken on forms of cultural xenophobia (in the wake of the war on terror and 9/11) directed at the Islamic subject, which have become a mainstay of the US imperial state in the context of postmillennial culture, and even more so in Trump's America.

Enemy Cuisines, Enemy Kitchens

For much of his artistic career, Michael Rakowitz, a multiracial artist of Iraqi Jewish origin, has turned to installation art and the sculptural mode in particular to initiate dialogue about what it means to imagine food as a way to bridge cultural difference. With the knowledge that the Iraqi is always already a nonsubject or an imagined enemy, in his work Rakowitz has aimed to think simultaneously about how to create a cultural dialogue in which Iraqi cuisine becomes legible and about how to share the legacy of his mother's recipes in a nation in which many people willfully refuse to see Iraqis and Iraqi Americans as viable human subjects. As part of an ongoing exploration of what it means to occupy the seemingly impossible position of being a Jewish Iraqi American, Rakowitz has staged three significant culinary-based social sculptures: *Enemy Kitchen* (2003–), *RETURN* (2004–), and *Spoils* (2011). In explaining the political and social issues that led him to want to use food as a possible way to think through social change, Rakowitz describes the power of witnessing protest. As cultural critic Ella Shohat notes, "According to Rakowitz, [*Enemy Kitchen*] gradually came about after he witnessed a long line of people waiting to eat in the Afghan restaurant Khyber Pass, in the East Village, New York, shortly after 9/11. In response to subsequent incidents of harassment, including the targeting of mosques and Muslim businesses, the people in line were demonstrating their support of the owners and staff of the restaurant."[13] When I read these words, I was struck by the notion that an intimate eating public of sorts had formed around this restaurant. In the wake of xenophobic sentiments levied against Afghan Americans and other Muslim Americans, restaurant goers had actively chosen to eat food from the provenance of the so-called enemy as an act of solidarity with Afghan immigrants in the US. What is more, Rakowitz's recollection of this moment reminded me of my own experience at Khyber Pass.

As I read Shohat's essay I recalled that back in 2001 I, too, had visited Khyber Pass. I had chosen to eat there because in my own way I wanted to support a restaurant that was serving food from an enemy nation. Although I can no longer recall what I ordered, what remains with me is a conversation I overheard at the restaurant. I distinctly remember sitting next to a queer couple. A part of their conversation led me to perk up in interest. Briefly, they were talking about how much they loved the flavors of Afghan food specifically and Middle Eastern food more broadly. One person at the table then said something to the effect of, "Just because they make good kebabs does not mean we should forgive them for what they did to us." That moment horrified me and made me fear for the safety of the restaurant owners. I do not recall whether the owners had placed a US flag in the window, as so many Muslim store owners were doing in 2001. But I do remember thinking that this moment perfectly encapsulated a prevailing sentiment in my life then—an idea that would find its way into my first book: even as cuisines may be desirable or even fetishized, the bodies that prepare those foods are often not welcome.

I had not thought about that moment until I read about Rakowitz's eerily parallel but divergent experience at Khyber Pass. At this critical juncture in 2021, I am struck by his very different experience at the restaurant when he witnessed the formation of an intimate eating public that was rallying against social injustice and thinking of ways that eating could be a political act to support a population under threat. My experience suggested something quite different—the notion that eating different food would not necessarily lead to a radical reorientation of political affinities.

Juxtaposing my experience at Khyber Pass with Rakowitz's is important because it underscores the importance of thinking through the instability of making meaning around food. Although it is possible for a form of radical kindness to emerge around a preference for Afghan food, it is also possible for forms of racism and xenophobia to emerge. Where Rakowitz witnessed kindness, I witnessed a stunning lack of generosity anchored in racism. Where Rakowitz saw strangers deliberately and strategically identifying other strangers as part of their intimate public, drawing lines of affiliation between diner and restaurateur, I saw strangers intent on maintaining a wall between diner and restaurateur. Where Rakowitz saw the stranger being transformed into a friend, I saw strangers being imagined as the enemy. As Sara Ahmed notes, strangers only become figures through their proximity to those who are deemed proper subjects of the nation—in this case, those who uphold forms of white supremacy and refuse to recognize the basic humanity of the Arab subject. Within certain discourses around neoliberal multiculturalism, some strangers are recognized as being part of the nation; indeed, it is when strange cultures are not only let into the nation but also redefined as part of the nation that we start to rethink how an intimate eating public can be defined through a politics of hope and optimism rather than exclusion alone. At the same time, other strangers can never be incorporated into the nation; the differences they possess—be they cultural, culinary, linguistic—are far too removed to become part of the nation. As Ahmed notes, this exclusion is part and parcel of the "double and contradictory process of incorporation and expulsion" within multiculturalism.[14] It thus becomes crucial for the nation to "differentiate between those strangers whose appearance of difference can be claimed by the nation, and those stranger strangers who may yet be expelled, whose difference may be dangerous to the well-being of even the most heterogeneous of nations."[15]

To this point, we might also take a page from Josephine Nock-Hee Park's argument about the "friendly." Drawing from the complex history of the US Cold War in Asia, Park adds nuance to the idea of what it means to occupy the position of racialized wartime ally when one is forever tainted by their proximity to the enemy. Park's compelling insight develops lines of thought from Jacques Derrida's *Politics of Friendship* in which he argues that "the friend and enemy pass through each other into one another."[16] Park argues that the context of the US Cold War means that "American friendship [has] always already been destabilized by imperial racism—and under this erasure, [the friend and the enemy are] rendered indistinct from the enemy: they, too, [are] existentially something different and alien. The friendly perpetually deconstructs the friend-enemy distinction to lay bare the politics of friendship."[17] Arguably, then, it is within this fissure of solidarity with the stranger and distance from the excessively strange stranger that Rakowitz's work emerges, inviting us to think about how we make meaning through, make community with, and form intimacies around food. It is around this idea of the "friendly" for those whom imperial forms of racism have seemingly dislodged any possibility of friendship that we start to think about altering the terms of intimacy and breaking bread together.

Rakowitz has repeatedly used his art to question how the stranger becomes an enemy and whether it is possible to use food to advance a conversation about who is imagined to be a legitimate member of the national imaginary and who, by extension, is castigated as the stranger or enemy who must be surveilled and kept at a safe distance. To follow the lead of Sita Kuratomi Bhaumik, an artist whose work I discussed at the beginning of this book, it is worth noting how food in the space of the social sculpture can be deployed for radically different purposes. In the case of an artist like Rirkrit Tiravanija, his first solo exhibit, titled *pad thai*, was an installation in which he transformed a gallery space into a kitchen and served pad thai to museum visitors. That exhibit, Bhaumik notes, was about articulating the ways "food places us in proximity with the other."[18] She goes on to note that Rakowitz's artistic oeuvre demands "intimacy with a contested identity, and opens dialogue about politics. . . . Tiravanija uses food to unite. Rakowitz uses food to incite."[19] Following this distinction between uniting and inciting, I suggest that Rakowitz's work invites us to engage with how inciting viewers and visitors to action is part and parcel of constructing this kind of intimate eating public, whereby politics is not diluted but brought to the forefront of each and every art installation. Ella Shohat notes:

> The culinary arena forms a significant theme in Rakowitz's engagement of Iraq. Projects such as Enemy Kitchen (Matbakh al-'adu) (2003–ongoing), RETURN (2004–ongoing), Spoils (2011), and Dar Al Sulh (Domain of Conciliation) (2013) entertain the production, consumption, and circulation of food. Whether in its raw materiality or in its refined display, the performance of food preparation comes to allegorize the politics of class, gender, religion, nation, and diaspora. Contrary to the exotica industry associated with Middle Eastern restaurants and cookbooks, Rakowitz's food projects comment on the transnational flow of images and sounds, of smells and tactile impressions intermingled with the ashes of war. Culinary memories are entangled with massive-scale, politically generated loss but also with the creative desire to survive in biological terms and regenerate in cultural terms.[20]

For Rakowitz, creating a critical context for imagining what Shohat describes as "politically generated loss" that leads to a "creative desire to survive" has meant that presenting Iraqi food and culture would necessarily take the form of a social sculpture.[21] Advanced by the artist Joseph Beuys, the idea of the "social sculpture" describes a participatory form of art in which the audience must willfully interact with the "art" object to actively generate meaning. That the capacity to be an artist is inherent in all beings runs central in Beuys's philosophy, and indeed to the work of the Fluxus movement of which he was a participant. For Beuys, to actively shape and be shaped by a work of art was part of the phenomenological experience of interacting with a work of art, be it an installation or performance. The art installation in Beuys's formulation is not about mediating direct knowledge but "produc[ing] deepened perceptions of experience . . . it is not there to be simply understood."[22]

Rakowitz's project emerges within this fissure between knowledge and experience as it pertains to the Iraqi subject, the subject of war, the "enemy" subject. Whereas *Enemy Kitchen* relies heavily on the cultural legacy created by the luxe lonchera that Arellano describes, Rakowitz's version of the food truck is far from being a gimmick. The gimmick, as Sianne Ngai notes, is that which can both charm and disturb us. The gimmick, particularly as it is attached to forms of late capitalism, is the thing we are drawn to because it approximates something of the novel and thus serves to attract us, but it is also off-putting insofar as it seems eventually to devolve into the realm of the tired cliché. If the gimmick, then, remains a gimmick—a thing not to be taken seriously—it is because it is seen to cheapen something to which noncapitalist value has been attached. Building on Ngai's work, I suggest that Rakowitz's culinary installations, and by extension the social sculpture, are as far from the gimmick as one can get. Rakowitz's culinary art is not about proliferating cuisines and creating the next new wave in the search for the novel in the landscape of the urban food truck movement. It is about a sustained engagement with puncturing one's experience with culinary sociality.[23]

Consider, for instance, the design of *Enemy Kitchen*. The actual food truck, a repurposed forty-year-old ice cream truck painted camouflage green, bears little resemblance to the typical food trucks that populate parking lots during food festivals or that one finds parked at curbsides late at night (figure 4.1). Instead, it looks eerily reminiscent of a military vehicle that would more naturally belong in the deserts of Fallujah carrying army personnel. Rakowitz's tongue-in-cheek reference to the truck as one that bears "weapons of mass deliciousness instead of mass destruction" addresses the deliberate use of combat and artillery to evoke the warscapes of Iraq, an image predominant in the mind of the mainstream US public, in large measure because of the constant scrutiny of the war-ravaged Iraqi landscape by the US news media.[24] *Enemy Kitchen*, as the project is named, was a mobile and multimedia art installation, produced in collaboration with Chicago's Smart Museum, aimed to disrupt the experience of the everyday through one's perception of what it means to eat the food of communities that have been discursively constructed as the "enemy" (figure 4.2). It prompts the question of what it means to eat from an enemy kitchen, which is a radically different way to pose a question of cultural encounter than asking what it means to break bread with and among friends.

Figure 4.1 *Enemy Kitchen*, a food truck in Chicago that features Iraqi refugee cooks and US veterans of the Iraq War as sous chefs. *Enemy Kitchen* is the city's first Iraqi restaurant to publicly declare itself as such. Image credit: Michael Rakowitz.

Figure 4.2 Food being served from the *Enemy Kitchen* food truck. Image credit: Michael Rakowitz.

As sociologist Alice Julier notes, meals are social events, and "people choose to participate in these events as a way of constructing close relationships that are not necessarily rooted in the obligations associated with kinship."[25]

And yet what does it mean when one accepts the food of the purported other while also remaining resolutely intolerant of the bodies and cultures from which the food originates? "Iraqi" cuisine, after all, is not easily imaginable within the virulently Islamophobic and anti-Arab context of the US. Rather, purveyors of Iraqi food in the United States must typically repackage their food as "Mediterranean" or "Lebanese"—and occasionally the more generic "Middle Eastern"—to avoid the stigma that comes from being marked as a purveyor of the "enemy's" cuisine. Moreover, the state-sanctioned limitations on Iraqi imports mean that food bearing the imprimatur of "made in Iraq" is carefully policed at the US border by Immigration and Customs Enforcement officials.

Part and parcel of RETURN, another art installation by Rakowitz, raises questions about how Iraqi foodstuffs such as dates travel to the US. Through this installation Rakowitz is able to probe the question of how the enemy is produced through food imports. In a description of the staging of RETURN, Hanae Ko notes, "On view at the store counter, where Rakowitz manned the desk, was paperwork filled out for US government agencies illustrating the near impossibility of international trade with Iraq even after the 2003 lifting of trade embargoes, in place since 1990."[26] In rendering visible the mechanisms of red tape and the deep legislative barriers to bringing dates to the United States, Rakowitz's exhibit obliges the public to consider why dates from Iraq have attained the dubious status of "enemy" food. To wrest the date from its origins in the Iraqi landscape is, in Rakowitz's view, a way to rewrite the history of this seemingly innocuous edible with a rather storied and embattled migration story. Analogously, in claiming the identity of the "enemy," Rakowitz's food truck asks diners to confront the terms under which their exchanges with multiculturalism are made palatable to themselves. To immerse oneself in the eating process while being cognizant of the narratives and histories of the foods in a nonsanitized form imbues this project with the radical potential to think more systematically about the plate of food one consumes.

In an artist statement about the origin of both *Enemy Kitchen* and RETURN, Rakowitz alludes to the "lack of Iraqi cultural visibility in the United States beyond the specter of war."[27] He goes on to tell a story about living and shopping in Brooklyn in August 2004. He describes patronizing the Sahadi Importing Co. on Atlantic Avenue. During one visit his eye is drawn to a can of date syrup and the label "Product of Lebanon" on the back. He notes his intrigue that this food (dates), which he knows as *silan* or *debes*, is considered Lebanese, because it features so prominently in many Iraqi dishes. He describes an interaction with the store owner that further complicates this seemingly simple statement of the date syrup's provenance:

> The owner Charlie Sahadi told me, "your mother is going to love this. It's from Baghdad." I looked at the label, which clearly stated Product of Lebanon. And that's when he told me that the date syrup is processed in the Iraqi capital, put into large plastic vats, and driven over the border into Syria where it is then taken across the border into Lebanon where it received a label for export to the rest of the world. From 1990 until May 2003, this was one method Iraqi companies used in order to circumvent UN sanctions. When I asked why it was still in practice in August 2004, more than a year after those sanctions had been dropped, Charlie replied that prohibitive charges—the result of the inevitable security scans by US Customs and Border Patrol and Homeland Security for any freight bearing the origin of Iraq—were to blame, and it was just too much of a risk.[28]

Rakowitz thus lays bare the mechanism by which "enemy" food comes into being. I use the term *enemy food* not as a catchy moniker, but to name the process by which foods of purportedly dubious origin must be repackaged in order to satisfy state surveillance mandates.

Although the pedagogic imperative of *Enemy Kitchen* operates at the level of the diner, it also operates within the kitchen. It emphasizes why we must think through the complex nexus of power that structures the lives of Iraqi restaurant workers who must often subordinate their racial and ethnic identities to the dictates of the xenophobic state that would prefer Iraqi refugees remain invisible. Rakowitz's project pairs Iraqi immigrants and refugees in the kitchen with US veterans of the Iraq War. As the artist Sita Kuratomi Bhaumik notes in her own article about Rakowitz's art, early sketches for *Enemy Kitchen* reveal a commitment to thinking about how the nation itself is imagined. Bhaumik notes that sketches for the project included two flags, "one to be raised when the truck was operated by a cook from Baghdad, another when operated by a cook from Iraqi Kurdistan, an autonomous region of Iraq"[29] (figure 4.3). She goes on to describe how members of Iraq Veterans against the War and Vietnam Veterans against the War worked as sous chefs and servers. Thus, in an attempt to invert the inherent dynamics that have

Truck with flag of Iraq displayed, when operated by a cook from Bagdad

Truck with Kurdish flag displayed, when operated by a cook from Iraqi Kurdistan.

Figure 4.3 Sketches for *Enemy Kitchen* noting how flags will indicate the national background of the chef. Image credit: Michael Rakowitz.

squarely placed power in the hands of US imperialist forces, Rakowitz creates a symbolic inversion by inviting the Iraqi refugees and immigrants to serve as chefs, with veterans serving as their sous chefs. That the veterans are in the position of figuratively being *sous*, under the power of the chef, taking orders from an Iraqi, is a performative gesture with tremendous rhetorical freight. In effect this hierarchy enacts the idea of the Cold War "friendly" that Park alludes to in *Cold War Friendships*. In this reversal lies a confrontation of the perpetual inequities that structure the lived realities within the warscape. As Mimi Nguyen points out, the refugee is often placed in a position of having to perform gratitude. Their acceptance in American society is marked by their willingness to perform gratefulness for American magnanimity, while also lessening bad feelings Americans may have about having invaded and destroyed the refugee's country.[30]

Through the continued and committed effort to link the process of making meaning—from food presentation, food preparation, to food's interface with the public—with larger questions about that which is viscerally uncomfortable, Rakowitz radically punctures the meaning of food truck meals. The food truck is not an object nouveau that exists within a comfortable part of a new neoliberal, multicultural world. Rather, it bears the traces of an ongoing war, serving as a reminder that food consumption and preparation are structured by profound asymmetries, and that food as art can offer profound pedagogic lessons.

And yet the pedagogic does not necessarily morph into the didactic in the sense that the meal is imagined as an invitation to a conversation, initiated by war, sustained by food, but not contained exclusively by the tribulations of war. In another art installation, Rakowitz collaborated with Kevin Lasko, chef at the New York City restaurant Park Avenue Autumn, to create a limited engagement event called *Spoils*, an implicit reference to the phrase *spoils of war*. As part of an elaborately crafted project, the restaurant opted to serve one of their courses on plates that had been looted from Saddam Hussein's palaces and eventually purchased via eBay. The dish of choice was a fusion of a traditional Iraqi dessert and a dinner entrée—date syrup and tahini topped with venison, pine nuts, and a chopped pomegranate garnish—expressly designed to confound both the palate and the diners (figure 4.4). Rakowitz notes, "I wanted to explore the tension between the diner's tongue, the delicious and sweet meal, and the bitter surface upon which it is presented. . . . Indeed, refusal, or the inability to eat or even order this dish because of the dishware's provenance or the circumstances under which it was acquired is just as important as the experience of consuming this dish."[31] By inviting diners to

Figure 4.4 *Spoils*, a culinary intervention in collaboration with Chef Kevin Lasko at Park Avenue Autumn, New York City. The dish features venison atop date syrup and tahini (*debes wa'rashi*) and is served on plates looted from Saddam Hussein's palaces. Image credit: Michael Rakowitz.

transform the dining experience into one that could be viscerally uncomfortable and necessarily discordant—at once an experience of delectable tastes coupled with a sense of defamiliarization in wondering what it means to eat off a plate from the collection of an infamous world leader—Rakowitz choreographs a meal that is as much about consumption as it is about refusal. But as Bhaumik notes, this edible text is one with an ending that "even the artist could not have scripted."[32]

A few days before the project was to end, the US State Department intervened and issued a cease-and-desist order in which Rakowitz and Lasko were asked to turn over the plates. The plates were to be authenticated and returned to Iraq. Notably, they were seized on December 14, 2011—the day before the conclusion of the Iraq War was announced. Although then president Barack Obama returned the plates to Iraqi Prime Minister Nouri al-Maliki, they lived on in another form in a retrospective of Rakowitz's art titled *Backstroke of the West*. When I visited the Museum of Contemporary Art in Chicago in 2018, I noticed a collection of objects from all of Rakowitz's art, designed, as the museum notes, to invite "viewers to contemplate their complicit relationship to the political world around them, recognizing that hospitality and hostility are interlinked."

In one corner of the exhibit hall, I noticed a stack of paper plates with an invitation for viewers to take one with them. Having seen images of the controversial plates that were the centerpiece of the meals served during the *Spoils* exhibit, I recognized that these paper plates were replicas of those original plates. I had read the sign inviting viewers to take a plate, but I could not help but feel I was crossing a line by taking a paper plate with me. I watched as other museumgoers looked at the photographs of the exhibit, picked up the paper plates, and then returned them to the stack. Nobody seemed to want to take one of the plates. I don't know whether it was because we are socialized to leave objects in a museum or because the plate itself produced a visceral reaction that made people not want to take it home once they learned the story behind its design. I was torn between knowing it was okay to take these plates and feeling like I was violating some imaginary rule. My solution was to stuff the plate into my oversized purse and take it home with me. In my own way, I had internalized the ideas of what this exhibit invited us to do—namely, to own how I was complicit with the political world in which I lived, even as the museum created a kind of intimate eating public through the curation of Rakowitz's work. The paper plate now sits on my bookshelf. It is a reminder to me both of the hospitality of Rakowitz's gesture and of how, as Bhaumik so eloquently notes about Rakowitz's oeuvre, "the edible text gains political power as it is consumed and shared."[33]

Serving up Culinary Conflict

Although the Pittsburgh-based restaurant Conflict Kitchen is not a food truck, I include an analysis of it alongside other forms of intimate eating publics not simply because it emerged at the same political-cultural moment that luxe loncheras were sweeping across the United States, but also because its objectives so closely align with disrupting the notion that consumption can be separated from the political conditions under which food is produced and distributed. Moreover, Conflict Kitchen is by its nature provisional and has its origins in art installation. The brainchild of multidisciplinary artists Jon Rubin and Dawn Weleski, Conflict Kitchen was a takeout-only restaurant that was open to the public from 2010 to 2017. As part of its novel approach to creating an engaged eating public, it altered its menu and storefront every four to six months. It has since stopped operating, but it used to function like a food truck in that it served a limited menu and was open only a few hours every day. In the years that Conflict Kitchen was operational, it relied heavily on the workings of social media—notably Facebook and Twitter—to build its customer base.[34]

During its operation, Conflict Kitchen was dedicated to serving the cuisine of countries or sovereign Indigenous territories with which the United States was engaged in military, diplomatic, or political conflict. Its particular national focus rotated a few times a year, and the establishment served up cuisine from nations such as North Korea, Iran, Cuba, Afghanistan, and Venezuela, as well as foods of Indigenous First Nations such as the Haudenosaunee Confederacy.[35] But the restaurant departed from tradition by not restricting its offerings to food alone. The restaurant did not solely focus on consumption, nor did it provide easy access to multicultural difference via a menu of rotating flavors.[36] It insistently focused on engaging the complex and lived realities of people whose lives are modulated by war, diplomacy, and violence. Rather than simply operating on a logic of seducing taste buds for the sake of novelty, the food served at the restaurant demanded an engagement with the voices of the people, communities, and cultures from which the food originated. The first point of contact at which this occurs is when one buys food from Conflict Kitchen. Food items come wrapped in a wrapper specially designed for each iteration; the wrappers are literally covered with the stories and voices of the people of that nation (figure 4.5). For instance, in one iteration of the

Figure 4.5 Close-up view of a disposable food wrapper from Conflict Kitchen.

restaurant, Cocina Cuba, the food was packaged in wrappers that included interviews with Cubans and Cuban Americans on topics ranging from culture to politics. As the Conflict Kitchen website notes, "As is to be expected, the thoughts and opinions that come through the interviews and our programming are often contradictory and complicated by personal perspective and history. These natural contradictions reflect a nuanced range of thought within each country and [serve] to instigate questioning, conversation, and debate with our customers."[37]

Recalling the assessment that Rakowitz's art is effective because it incites rather than unites allows us to see points of convergence between *Enemy Kitchen* and Conflict Kitchen. The fact that the Conflict Kitchen food wrapper obliges consumers to linger, perhaps even to save it as a souvenir, runs counter to the typical notion that once one has consumed, one does not have to think any more about the food. Jon Rubin notes, "We want people to think about places in a different light. . . . Our goal, we often say, is not to simplify but to actually complicate it. For us, we want to provoke them but also to *seduce* them. The food is there to seduce, but then we want to instigate a nuanced, engaged discussion that we're often times ashamed to have in public."[38] The wrapper then becomes an object of engaged performance. It is at once a narrative about culture, politics, everyday life, and food. It is also a narrative about what typically goes unsaid within the space of the alimentary exchange. By not shying away from what I have elsewhere described as the unpalatable, the wrapper becomes a multivalent object that speaks to a complex history that is not so easily disposed and discarded, implicitly countering a culture of fast food wherein waste is generated amid an ethos of disposable junk.

Although its menu was relatively sparse, as might be expected from a small establishment—another facet that made Conflict Kitchen comparable to a food truck—the restaurant extended the walls of its space further than those of a typical restaurant. In addition to serving food in its strategically designed wrappers, at once objects of useable, diplomatic, everyday art and a mode of exchange, Conflict Kitchen also pushed the envelope when it comes to thinking about what kinds of conversations can happen within the space of a restaurant. Per their mission statement: "Conflict Kitchen uses the social relations of food and economic exchange to engage the general public in discussions about countries, cultures, and people that they might know little about outside of the polarizing rhetoric of governmental politics and the narrow lens of media headlines. In addition, the restaurant creates a constantly changing site for ethnic diversity in the post-industrial city of Pittsburgh, as it has presented the only Iranian, Afghan, Venezuelan, North Korean, Haudenosaunee, and Palestinian restaurants the city has ever seen."[39]

Offered alongside the rotating menus was a series of events designed to harness the potential of web communication apps such as Skype to promote dialogue and conversation about the cultures in conflict, moving beyond the simple rhetoric of "axis of evil" pervasive within the mainstream media. During the restaurant's first iteration, it took on the form of an Iranian restaurant named Kubideh Kitchen. As part of its public programming, Conflict Kitchen hosted a virtual dinner connecting diners in Pittsburgh and Tehran. Using webcam technologies, diners took part in what was described as an "international dinner party." Those in Tehran ate the same food—chicken stew with pomegranate and walnuts; a beef stew with dried limes and greens; and crusty, bottom-of-the-pot rice—as their counterparts in Pittsburgh. With the notion that food could serve, literally and metaphorically, as a means of breaking bread, the conversation began with discussions about how Iranians purchase their bread. As Riddhi Shah notes, the conversation then "veer[ed] into the related topic of growing your own herbs (almost a universal practice in Iran) and eventually morph[ed] into an edgier discussion about dating and politics and larger commonalities—two young graduates talked about the difficulty of finding a job after getting their college degrees."[40] In turn the Americans in the United States at the meal shared their stories, thereby setting up a reciprocal dynamic in which the US participants served as native informants about US culture for the non-US cooks and eaters. For Dawn Weleski, one of the restaurant owners, food has the function of establishing a common ground mediated in the possibility that people can "find commonality in their experiences through the way the food smells and tastes."[41] In this way, a provisional but important eating public was formed among diners in Tehran and Pittsburgh.

On December 6, 2013, I had the opportunity to participate in one of these curated public eating events. Along with seven other participants from around the world, I joined the organizers of Conflict Kitchen, Dawn Weleski in Anyang, South Korea, and Jon Rubin in Pittsburgh, on Skype for a synchronous lesson on cooking North Korean cuisine led by Yeonji Cho, an experienced chef and North Korean defector who had moved to Seoul, South Korea. The "North Korean Cooking Lesson" was a collaboration jointly undertaken by the Anyang Public Art Project, an organization that uses public art to help reimagine how citizens make sense of their city and that creates larger conversations about public art and new media, as well as Jogakbo, a human rights group focused on North Korea–related issues.[42]

On this particular evening, we prepared *soegogi-muguk* (beef and radish soup) and *gamjajeon* (potato pancakes). We were asked to prepare our *mise en place* ahead of time and then start cooking in our kitchens, keeping a Skype window open and the webcam trained on what we were doing. When that was done, we all sat in front of our screens and ate our meal together, talking about North Korean life, politics, and food. When all was said and done the event was edited and uploaded to Vimeo for all to see.[43] Keeping in mind that this meal took place in 2013, well before the COVID-19 pandemic made synchronous meals via web-based platforms like Skype, Zoom, and Webex commonplace, this kind of intimacy within this public space requires a radical rethinking of the possibility of temporal, diplomatic, and conceptual distance between purported enemies.

During its run, Conflict Kitchen hosted several other meals, either in person or as virtual synchronous events via Skype, during which diners from different nation-states would share stories and implicitly take on the role of native informant. And yet no two meals were exactly the same. The ephemeral nature of each meal and the difference in the questions posed by participants render it performance-like. Each iteration is unique and creates a unique set of interpersonal connections, contradictions, and conversations. Not easily reproducible, each dinner event becomes like an art installation in which food is used as a platform to initiate critical dialogue enabled by a form of radical hospitality, which ultimately also invites and incites diners to think about how to effect radical change.

Culinary Diplomacy and Alternative Epistemologies of the Intimate

Lest one think that all forms of performative-based food trucks are necessarily politically enabling or capable of enacting radical hospitality, I turn now to a much more quotidian example of one documentary's narrative about a Pakistani immigrant who operates a food cart in Manhattan. Despite the food truck's apparent ability to reinvent itself endlessly, it has long been the mainstay of the immigrant and working class. It has been both operated by the working class and patronized by the working class. Ramin Bahrani's remarkable short neorealist film, *Man Push Cart* (2005), provides a radically unsentimental portrayal of life for the typical food truck worker. As it follows the workday of New York City food vendor Ahmad, the film focuses on the quotidian reality of being a food cart vendor. Ahmad's work consists of backbreaking labor, long hours, and indifferent customers. The foods he sells are not a mashup of fusion cuisine but staples of the New York commuting class—donuts, bagels, coffee. Little distinguishes him from the scores of vendors of color who sell food every day on the corners of busy streets of New York City. Indeed, in his need to blend in, his clothing is deliberately nonexotic; he wears a hoodie and jeans, fading into the background. In a notable scene in the film we see him prepare his cart for the day's work. As a pushcart vendor, he must be set up for work to be able to feed morning commuters looking to grab a quick donut, coffee, or bagel on their way into the office, so he is up early to prepare, long before the city has begun to awaken from slumber. The film zeroes in on his hard work. We see him visibly breathless as he labors to push the heavy cart through Manhattan, sometimes up inclines, stopping and starting in order to navigate the ebb and flow of traffic and red lights.[44]

Ahmad's life is not structured by a desire to make his cuisine or his culture visible—he does not have that luxury. As Junaid Rana notes, Ahmad's life is one of "downward mobility" in which he toils to pay his debts.[45] There is nothing performative about his food cart. There is nothing "ethnic" on display. He is not using his pushcart or the food he sells to try to lay bare the economic, political, and social inequities that define the life of the Pakistani Muslim migrant. As Rana notes, Ahmad lives in a world "in which migrants are trapped by the difficult work conditions, exploitative economic relationships, loneliness, racism and the social marginalization that surrounds them."[46] Ahmad instead must work tirelessly to make ends meet.

The economic reality structuring this film's depiction of the food cart vendor stands in contrast to the possibilities for culinary and cultural diplomacy that I have described in spaces like Enemy Kitchen and Conflict Kitchen. If one is the embodiment of the purported enemy—the "terrifying Muslim," to use Junaid Rana's term—one wields considerably less cultural capital amid a world in which the mobile dining scene can become an occasion to synesthetically produce a different kind of eating experience that conjures a new kind of intimate eating public. Ultimately, the narrative produced in Man Push Cart also stands in stark contrast to the narrative produced by the glamorized food truck of Chef. Ahmad's bodily labor demands that he work tirelessly to become part of an invisible workforce, and yet the kind of work he does has no cultural payoff—he does not ascend through the culinary ranks, nor does he gain any kind of recognition for his work. As Alison Caldwell notes, street food vending has historically provided immigrants without access to credit and cultural capital a "foothold into the American dream."[47] The emerging microblogging food vendor population (depicted in *Chef*) is predominantly nonimmigrant and has greater access to forms of cultural capital. They can be successful precisely because of their greater access to a wider range of cultural narratives and forms of mobility.

To return to the main focus of this chapter, both Conflict Kitchen and *Enemy Kitchen* produce a very strategic kind of culinary narrative. Harnessing the potential that food has to create social change, the narratives lodged within each remain optimistic about the transformative potential of eating in public and forms of stranger intimacy. What is more, these eating publics are created in provisional spaces and among strangers. The occasion of eating together is not about avoiding difficult questions or hard conversations; to the contrary, it is about thinking through the juxtaposition of enjoying a meal while also working through difficult and often unpalatable topics. These public spaces of culinary intimacy are about imagining ways to work through difficulty but outside of the mechanisms of state or formal forms of regulation. In this way, the careful curation of these spaces can be seen, to follow Gayatri Gopinath, as acts of queer curation. They bring together unlikely friends to destabilize the machinations of neoliberal multiculturalism.

As Sita Kuratomi Bhaumik astutely notes about Michael Rakowitz's art—his desire to use art to incite rather than unite—rarely is his work motivated by a desire to provide easy answers. She notes, "while the presence of Iraqi food in American social spheres can begin to remedy our ignorance about Iraqi culture, Rakowitz is not naïve. In his art practice, breaking bread is not a panacea for war wounds."[48] As such, these art installations stand in contrast to the forms of culinary diplomacy that were strategically institutionalized through specific State Department programs under the direction of former presidential candidate and former secretary of state Hillary Rodham Clinton. Although it is perhaps unsurprising that the Donald Trump regime eliminated it, the rhetorical and ideological freight of the Diplomatic Culinary Partnership bears discussion in the context of my elaboration on forms of radical hospitality and culinary diplomacy.[49]

Under the Obama administration, food justice took center stage for a short time. When former First Lady Michelle Obama launched her Let's Move! campaign and began using the south lawn of the White House to create a vegetable garden, food became a topic of serious discussion worthy of national attention.[50] During the Obama administration, food politics spread from the White House to the State Department, where it became a diplomatic instrument under an initiative known as the Diplomatic Culinary Partnership program (hereafter DCP), developed in conjunction with the James Beard Foundation. The White House created the American Chef Corps, a group of chefs who acted as "food-focused statesmen, dispatched around the globe to promote American cuisine and ingredients."[51] The DCP was officially launched at the US Department of State in 2012, largely at the behest of Secretary of State Hillary Clinton's passion and belief that better and more effective diplomacy happens over a dining table rather than a conference table. Clinton's efforts at institutionalizing culinary diplomacy were about effecting policy level change, but it is worth noting how the rhetoric of the program recalls the implicit ideas that structure Conflict Kitchen and *Enemy Kitchen*. Capricia Penavic Marshall, former chief of protocol under the Obama administration, notes that "by showcasing the best of American cuisine and creativity, we can show our guests a bit about ourselves . . . . Likewise, by incorporating elements of our visitor's culture, we can demonstrate respect and a desire to connect and engage. The connections formed over a shared meal can develop into some of the strongest bonds."[52] Here we see how the focus is trained on achieving unity, rather than seeking to incite, through these State Department–sponsored meals. Although the DCP is no longer active, its brief existence speaks to the powerful ways in which food was being imagined as a tool of diplomacy that could create the kind of intimate eating public that foregrounded the political work food was capable of doing, albeit within the realm of public policy.

In this chapter, I have gestured toward ways to read the food truck in the current neoliberal multicultural moment as a multivalent signifier that allows us to imagine more intimate ways to broker culinary diplomacy. Outside of the traditional lines of public policy, these kinds of art installations remind us about the possibilities for social change that can emerge from the construction of informal and provisional intimate eating publics. At the same time, much as we might remain optimistic about the possibilities of the food truck as a vehicle for engaging and initiating social dialogue, we must remain vigilant about thinking about what it means for the bodies that actually depend on the food truck or food cart as a livelihood. Within this aesthetic-critical space—as evinced from *Enemy Kitchen* and Conflict Kitchen—are opportunities to think about how and what one eats. To that end, the social sculpture, with its insistence on radical forms of hospitality, remains salient. Further, one can usefully reflect on what the figure of the enemy combatant embodies and what the construction of these radical eating publics, however temporary or provisional, can add to this important critical conversation.

People like me who came to England in the 1950s have been there for centuries; symbolically, we have been there for centuries. I was coming home. I am the sugar at the bottom of the English cup of tea. I am the sweet tooth, the sugar plantations that rotted generations of English children's teeth. There are thousands of others beside me that are, you know, the cup of tea itself. Because they don't grow it in Lancashire, you know. Not a single tea plantation exists within the United Kingdom. This is the symbolization of English identity—I mean, what does anybody in the world know about an English person except that they can't get through the day without a cup of tea? Where does it come from? Ceylon—Sri Lanka, India. That is the outside history that is inside the history of the English. There is no English history without that other history.
—Stuart Hall, "Old and New Identities"

In the opening pages of Kamila Shamsie's *Home Fire*, Isma, a young Pakistani British woman headed to the US for university studies, is detained by airport security at Heathrow Airport in London. During the interrogation, the customs officer asks Isma to establish her Britishness. In particular he asks her whether she considers herself British. "I am British," she asserts. "But do you consider yourself British?" he asks.[1] Isma responds to his query by noting that she has lived in London her whole life. Yet it soon becomes clear that Isma has to demonstrate her Britishness via a set of expectations that place less importance on her domicile and more emphasis on her affective relationship to Britishness. To be British and Muslim, Isma learns, one cannot just live in Britain. One must display a set of attitudes that include loyalty to the crown. Thus, a good British subject must denounce suicide bombers and the invasion of Iraq, and have a prepared answer about the Shia and the Sunni. But a certain levity is introduced into the conversation when Isma is asked to display a form of cultural literacy about British popular culture in the late 2010s. As part of a lengthy interrogation to ascertain Isma's affective claim to Britishness, Isma is asked to share her feelings about *The Great British Bake Off* (hereafter *GBBO*).[2]

And yet both Isma and her sister, Aneeka, wholly expect such interrogation. As Isma prepares to leave for the US and to navigate UK Border Force, she and Aneeka run through the possible questions she may encounter. Shamsie notes, "The interrogation continued for nearly two hours. He wanted to know her thoughts on Shias, homosexuals, the Queen, democracy, *The Great British Bake Off*, the invasion of Iraq, Israel, suicide bombers, dating websites."[3]

It is not enough that she is British; she must *feel* it. And feeling British in this context means having the correct answers. Isma must, in essence, follow a certain script about the contours of affective citizenship and publicly share her purported feelings about this form of belonging with the border security agent. Her performance of Britishness is of the utmost necessity if she is to viably be allowed to pass freely through the borders of the nation.

Anyone who has been interrogated at length by officers of the Transportation Security Administration in the US, or UK Border Force, knows that *being* a citizen is not the same as being *accepted* as one. To be read as properly of a place, one must—as Shamsie's novel lays bare—be aware that a certain kind of script establishes that one belongs in Britain. For Isma, this expectation means she must be fluent in the language of popular culture. It is notable that the agent does not ask Isma whether she likes to bake or cook; rather, he wants to know whether she imagines herself to be part of a larger national collective who will sit down in front of the television each week to watch one of the most beloved television shows of the post-2010s. As Benedict Anderson reminds us, for a nation to hold itself together, its citizens must imagine themselves as a community. A "deep horizontal comradeship"—what we might imagine as a feeling of kinship and intimacy—must exist for the people who comprise the nation.[4] Anderson notes that "communities are to be distinguished, not by their falsity/genuineness, but by the style in which they are imagined."[5] If print capitalism was the glue that bound the nation together in the early twentieth century, watching certain kinds of television shows, such as *GBBO*, is the linchpin that keeps the nation in place today. This latter point speaks to the issue of how Isma establishes her Britishness.

To merely declare that one has lived in Britain for all one's life is not enough. Isma must render entirely clear that she is part of the community via the style that Britain is an imagined community. She describes as a "slip" the moment during which she claims she *is* British but does not think to clarify that she *feels* British. She is quick to note that she corrects her error and returns to the script she and her sister had practiced in preparation for her imminent trip. Practicing how to successfully navigate the security screening process demands that the unruly body (marked by its racial, sexual, or gendered difference) be able to fit into a palatable narrative of the requirements of citizenship. For Isma, a young woman who wears hijab, the best way she can demonstrate her Britishness is to be able to enter into a discussion about the nation's most beloved cooking show.

As the scene progresses, we learn that Isma, ably assisted by Aneeka, has prepared answers for the inevitable questions she now has to answer. She runs through the possible answers for more politically charged questions, and she feels triumph when she hears a question for which she has at the ready a scripted answer. But of note in this section of Shamsie's novel is the idea that GBBO is an indelible marker of Britishness. In the following extract we see the ways in which the sisters rehearse the answers to produce an acceptable script:

> *You know, you don't have to be so compliant about everything,* Aneeka had said during the role-playing. Isma's sister, not quite nineteen, with her law student brain, who knew everything about her rights and nothing about the fragility of her place in the world. *For instance, if they ask you about the Queen, just say, "As an Asian I have to admire her color palette."* *It's important to show at least a tiny bit of contempt for the whole process.* Instead, Isma had responded, *I greatly admire Her Majesty's commitment to her role.* But there had been comfort in hearing her sister's alternative answers in her head, her *Ha!* of triumph when the official asked a question that she'd anticipated and Isma had dismissed, such as the *Great British Bake Off* one.[6]

How one feels about the show is as important as how one feels about much more hallowed British traditions such as the monarchy, democracy, and the growing presence of Muslim immigrants. Indeed, to establish oneself as unequivocally British means that one must implicitly aver that they devote an hour each week to the national pastime—watching a group of Britons assemble under a white tent to bake.

As I draw this book and its discussion of intimate eating publics to a close, I examine how the immensely popular GBBO emerges within the provisional space of the white baking tent where a group of ten to twelve home cooks from across Britain gather each week to bake all manner of sweets and savories. Not home, not office, and not restaurant, the tent is yet another space in which networks of affiliation, though provisional, serve to construct an image of a nation that establishes and renews its links in the intimate public sphere. On the show the nation becomes an intimate space wherein baking together forms the basis of a shared vision of the future, one that runs contrary to the ideas of a separationist UK in a post-Brexit era.[7]

Although the home bakers themselves are important to this vision of a nation in which centrifugal forces bring people together, the baking ingredients also establish the ethos of this nation's imaginary. In GBBO's construction of a multicultural, postcolonial utopia away from the realities of an exclusionary post-Brexit UK, race plays an important part in defining what can be baked into quintessentially British fare. To this end, I pay close attention to the role of the South Asians who have appeared on the show (notably Nadiya Hussain and Rahul Mandal), and how race and sensory difference play an important role in creating a sense of comfort on the popular baking show. I show how South Asian spices have a special place in the history of GBBO; every season, bakers have attempted to fuse curries, masalas, and chutneys with traditional fare. The judge Paul Hollywood usually responds with a skeptical raised brow at the thought of a curry-infused soggy bottom, but some of the judges also convey excitement at the prospect of a successful dish that would represent the "ethnic" flavors and spices of Britain's former colonies. The domestication of Indian ingredients in UK kitchens and pantries, however, also requires that we consider which aspects are rendered assimilable and able to enhance the flavor of British baked goods versus the kinds of pungent spices that are more likely to raise the eyebrows of the skeptical Paul and his co-judges, Mary Berry for the first several seasons and later Prue Leith.[8]

In terms of understanding how the show operates, it is worth asking why a show like this emerged in Britain at this particular moment. At a time when the UK is all but inclusive, it is no wonder that an imagined and inclusive nation is being created on television that is at odds with what is happening in the UK at the time.[9] Moreover, the show and its construction of an affective intimacy has relied on creating a kind of loving reality in which a kinder, gentler version of Britishness is accessible via reality television. But of course this "reality" is still a commodified one, even as it seems to temper the bad feelings that emanate from the current political climate. Indeed, the kind of coziness that the show not just produces but celebrates in the signature marquee works as a momentary salve from the negative affects of an increasingly inward-looking xenophobic nationalism that does not want immigrants or difference.[10] Since it began airing in 2010, the show has insistently emphasized that it is a different kind of cooking show and a different kind of reality show.[11] Working against a vision of competitiveness, it imagines a space and possibility for rivals on the show to compete against one another but also to root for one another. Here, then, we see how the contestants are simultaneously competitors and friends; they exist in intimate tension with one another to work through the tense pressures of making cakes—Will gels set in time? Will cakes be cool enough to allow frosting to stay in place?—and the competitive nature of the baking show to nevertheless remain committed to each other's success.[12]

Individual bakers of immigrant backgrounds, such as Nadiya Hussain, Tamal Ray, and Rahul Mandal, are as much a part of this imagined space of inclusive Englishness as more stereotypically white English home bakers who regularly make classic British tray bakes. Take for example the final episode of season 6 when Nadiya is announced winner.[13] Although we see the requisite shots of Nadiya's family feeling elated when they hear her declared the winner, we also see a telling moment at the end, when fellow South Asian and runner-up Tamal Ray stops to talk to Nadiya's small children. The camera zooms in to capture Tamal crouching down as he says, "I think I'm going to come around to your house at some point in the next few weeks and we're going to have dinner. Yeah? Okay? Your mummy's promised me." As he stands up, wiping tears from his face (it's unclear whether these are tears of sadness for having lost or tears of joy for Nadiya), he speaks directly to the camera and says, "Baking with a group of people you get on with so well and that you feel so proud for them when they do well, [sobbing] it's just . . . yeah it's just amazing." Throughout the season the show emphasizes the closeness among the two. Tamal and Nadiya are presented not as rivals, but as supportive allies who will continue their friendship after the camera stops rolling. Significantly, fans watching the show were aware of Tamal's queerness, and so the friendship that emerged over the show dovetailed with the not-uncommon pairing of coupled straight women establishing intimate bonds of kinship with their best gay friend.

Throughout the series, a number of similar friendships and bonds of kinship are highlighted. In this sense the show works toward an aspirational vision of the nation. Beyond the policies of Cool Britannia of the 1990s is the reality in which the contestants of the 2010s exist. Out there, beyond the white marquee tent, the show seems to suggest, Britain may be moving toward exclusionary politics that would seek to sever the links the nation has with difference and even rid Britain of the kinds of Black British contestants that are so beloved on the show. Inside the tent, however, is a newer and kinder nation—an intimate eating public in which the members of the nation bake together to imagine a better future for a nation riven by exclusion and division. It is at once predicated on a kind of false nostalgia for a happier, gentler time and invested in the idea of a future culinary utopia.

It is notable that the contestants themselves are attuned to the possibilities the show traffics in, particularly the ways in which the show seemingly provides a salve against the realities of a nation increasingly hostile to otherness. I was fascinated to read that Chetna Makan, who participated in season 5 of the show, is quite cognizant of this particular logic. As a South Asian immigrant contestant (though not as famous as winners Nadiya Hussain and Rahul Mandal), she was one of the first on the show to bring Indian flavors into the weekly bakes. As noted in a *New York Times* article about the show's embrace of multiculturalism, Makan lauds GBBO for providing a space to suffuse staid British classics with the flavors and tastes of an immigrant palate:

> "Every week I tried to bake something with flavors that maybe Mary and Paul hadn't tasted," [Makan] said. "I really wanted them to fall in love with what I made." In fact, she further notes that being on the show is "'the opposite of Brexit.'" "It's so different from the picture 'Brexit' painted, that the British want their nation back and that they want us out," she said. That's not how it actually feels, Ms. Makan said, both in the tent and outside of it. "It was the most welcoming, warm place, that showed unity and love among the competitors," she said. "The 'Bake Off' has had such a positive effect on people's lives, certainly for the people on the show, but also for the people watching."[14]

Here, then, Makan succinctly articulates how GBBO has been so successful in its ability to reimagine the nation. The space of GBBO is imagined as a postcolonial utopia, but it is also set in an idealized version of England: home bakers of all ages and races work together in a bucolic landscape under a pleasant white marquee tent with Union Jack bunting. On the show, the camera pans from close-ups of baking in progress to the occasional shot of an English flower, a bird nesting on a branch, or some other singular feature of the pastoral English landscape. As some have noted, the show goes so far as to produce its own version of royalty. Mary Berry, one of the lead judges of the show, presides over the show as a signifier of the monarchy. Peri Bradley notes, "With her received pronunciation and being almost as old as the Queen, she possesses a similar bearing of power and authority, albeit in the field of cooking rather than sovereignty."[15] This version of Englishness is one around which a multicultural nation rallies. It palpably drips with nostalgia for an imagined, affectively inclusive past. And yet in contrast to this vision of how an intimate eating public can form around baking while also staving off the ever-growing pressures of xenophobia is the reality of the very real structural racism that reminds us that the GBBO's vision of a happy, multicultural Britain is, ultimately, a utopic one.

Each episode of GBBO is divided into three segments, each with its own challenge. Moreover, each one is devoted to a different kind of baked good—breads, cakes, savories, those made with alternate flours, and so on. Bakers must successfully navigate each challenge if they are to make it through to the next episode. Each episode begins with the "signature" challenge, which is followed by a "technical" challenge, and concludes with the "showstopper." The signature bake is designed to allow bakers to display their skill and adeptness with basic recipes that they've often pretested at home. These are typically British staples such as cakes, biscuits, breads. Bakers are invited—even encouraged—to add their own personal touches. In season 6, the one in which Nadiya Hussain finally secured the win, the signature bake in episode 1, a madeira cake, saw the show's two South Asian contestants, Nadiya and Tamal, prepare an orange and green cardamom cake and a rose and pistachio cake, respectively. During the ninth season, the eventual winner, Rahul Mandal, made coriander posto and roasted vegetables rose tartlets and ghugni chaat tartlets for the vegan episode, during which bakers were asked to make eight signature vegan tartlets.

The technical challenge requires contestants to demonstrate their ability to perfectly mimic classics. With no prior knowledge of what they will be baking, they are given a partial recipe and expected to rely on their technical knowledge to reproduce perfectly whatever task has been set before them. Florentines, ciabattas, *kouign-amann*, and Victoria sandwiches were just some of the challenges during season 5.

Finally, the showstopper challenge requires bakers to produce over-the-top creations that are both wildly imaginative and fantastical and often require great precision and skill. These have included such challenges as a "3D biscuit selfie," "spiced biscuit chandeliers," and three-tier flower cakes. Here again, contestants often accent their bakes with touches of the immigrant palate:

for her 3D bread challenge, Nadiya Hussain created a snake charmer's box; in the challenge to make vol-au-vents, Nadiya's included Bengali korma and clementines; and for the biscuit chandelier challenge, South Asian contestants Rahul and Ruby made a Durga Puja chandelier and a peacock chandelier, respectively.

With a vision of difference baked into the contestants' confections, the show thus celebrates the differences that Indian spices and designs can bring to the traditional British (and occasionally European) bake. But this acceptance is often only a very surface-level embrace of difference. As Stuart Hall notes in the epigraph to this chapter, the history of British empire—particularly the cup of tea—is indelibly connected with a history of imperialism.[16] As Hall makes clear, the ultimate symbol of Englishness, a cup of tea, cannot exist without thinking about colonial intimacies linking India, China, the Caribbean, and the UK. Tea and sugar are commodities that entered the British diet via colonial exploitation in the aforementioned spaces, and yet a strategic amnesia covers over that history in favor of a more sanitized version of history. And yet, interestingly, although the initial seasons of GBBO often attempted to chronicle a history of baking, tracing the origins of the Bakewell tart or medieval game pies via brief historical interludes, none of the short historical musings reflect on the history of the spice trade or how sugar and flour came to exist in Britain's pantries. Nonetheless, sugar and tea are commodities that drive the British nation, both in terms of its economy and the development of its cuisine. This "outside" history is contained within the history of the English, yet it is completely forgotten in the nation's pull toward amnesiac imaginings of the homogeneously unified nation.

To take Edward Said's lead in *Culture and Imperialism*, one may usefully place a show like GBBO alongside a novel like *Mansfield Park*. For Said, it is important to see how Austen's novel nudges readers toward seeing the historical intimacies between sugar production in Antigua, Britain's slave trade, and the possibilities afforded to the Bertram family back on their family estate in England. The Bertrams, Said notes, "would not have been possible without the slave trade, sugar and the colonial planter class."[17] For Said, the task of the critic is to make connections, "to read what is there or not there, above all, to see complementarity and interdependence instead of isolated, venerated or formalized experience that excludes and forbids the hybridized intrusions of human history."[18] For even as references to these historical intimacies may remain more of a casual order in Austen's work, it is necessary for readers to see that the novel implicitly accesses these histories of colonialism. As such, a practice of reading and viewing GBBO that does not think about the provenance of the ingredients that allow forms of British baking to emerge fails to seize upon the vital ways in which baking is also built on forms of complementarity and interdependence that are also rooted in histories of colonial violence and exploitation.

Ultimately the show espouses a very happy-go-lucky version of multiculturalism wherein all ingredients can be added without reflection on the material and historical realities that account for how these goods exist in English home pantries. Take, for example, the first episode devoted exclusively to dairy, the fourth episode of the seventh season. As part of the showstopper challenge, contestants were asked to prepare *mishti*, a Bengali dessert of fermented sweet yogurt. Although seemingly inclusive of the possibility that Indian desserts can find a place at the gingham altar, little effort is made to contextualize the provenance of mishti or its constituent ingredient, *khoya*. Rather, mishti takes its place alongside all manner of British desserts, with little attention given to the colonial intimacies that make it possible to imagine mishti or khoya within this particular conjuring of Britishness.

It is to this logic of enfolding former colonial intimacies into the vision of the nation that "The Great Brexit Bake Off" speaks. In this short creative piece that appeared in the pages of the *New Yorker*, Krithika Varagur lampoons the show's characteristic baking challenges by imagining a series of alternative challenges that speak to the vagaries of the contemporary post-Brexit ethnic and racial climate. In the piece, Varagur provides a mock-up of four imagined episodes, describing the baking challenges each home baker must face. In summarizing the challenges, Varagur—in no uncertain terms—articulates food with contemporary British politics. Consider the description of episode 1, Breads:

Episode 1: Breads

Signature Challenge
Bake any flatbread that originated in a country that was once part of the British Empire.

Technical Challenge
Make two loaves of banana bread with the ingredient quantities, as specified in the traditional recipe, scaled to take into account the increased cost of bananas and sugar if Britain exits the European common market and is subjected to twenty-two-per-cent World Trade Organization tariffs.

Showstopper Challenge

[Make] a loaf of Irish soda bread imprinted with some schematic representation of the—currently demilitarized, but who knows for how long—Irish border.[19]

In her discussion of how celebrity functions on *GBBO* to recruit a nation driven by "negative affects like rage, hate and disgust," Jorie Lagerwey notes how the positive affects and emotions performed on the show rotate around a kind of love that "offers a direct contrast to those harsh contemporary realities by re-creating an imagined nation that is inclusive, diverse, and offers equal opportunity for Britons across regions, ages, sexualities, classes, races and ethnicities."[20] Varagur's satirical piece reminds us of how the show traffics in this palatable version of reality by honing in on the fact that the provenance of food is never neutral.

Of note in the above is the fact that baking has a history rooted in imperialism. The signature challenge, for instance, lays bare that the cast of characters who populate the show are often immigrants or descendants of immigrants from Britain's former colonies. The discussion of the technical challenge in Varagur's piece addresses the very real changes that, at the time of this writing, will likely be wrought on the nation as the UK follows through with Brexit desires to leave the European Union. At the same time, the showstopper speaks to the *longue durée* of the historical tensions between Ireland and the UK. In this way, the satirically oriented piece drives home the idea that *GBBO* deliberately and strategically refuses to see a continuity between contemporary exclusionary politics and the form of cultural amnesia it produces by imagining an inclusive and happy British nation.

We would do well to remember that, as Lucy Potter and Claire Westall note in an article about the austerity foodscape in neoliberal multicultural Britain, "the 'Bake Off' capitalises upon an imperially-rooted presentation of Britain's saleable version of pastoral Englishness, offering pseudo-colonial fairplay claims alongside cricketing countryside visuals and re-uniting the nostalgic 'charms' of British bunting with English village tea-parties and countrified kitchen aesthetics."[21] Despite the inclusion and celebration of the postcolonial immigrants who win the show with some regularity—or who, at the very least, emerge as fan favorites—*GBBO* not only relies on but also produces an amnesia of imperialism and resurrects nostalgia for a pastoral English past, a salve against Brexit-era England in the construction of this version of an intimate public. Here, stranger intimacy becomes possible and even celebrated because of an investment in the idea of a better good life. In this utopic vision of a better good life for Britain, people of different races and ethnicities compete against one another but do so in a spirit of comradery that, on the surface, challenges the inevitable pull of xenophobic racism that is endemic to the bad feelings of late capitalism. In this postcolonial utopia, in this intimate eating public, time slows even as contestants race to make better and more delicious baked foods than their competitors.

Indeed, it is precisely the emphasis on time as a value of late-stage capitalism that has made cooking shows so popular in Britain. Where cooking shows often celebrate the emergence of elaborate meals, they also drive home the idea that time is money and that well-prepared meals can be made quickly within the home. This version of domestic coziness reminds us that despite a value on lingering over and savoring food, late-stage capitalism ultimately counts on a logic of food and commodities being prepared quickly. As Karl Marx notes, "Capitalist production is not merely the production of commodities, it is essentially the production of surplus-value. The labourer produces, not for himself, but for capital. It no longer suffices, therefore, that he should simply produce. He must produce surplus-value. That labourer alone is productive, who produces surplus-value for the capitalist, and thus works for the self-expansion of capital."[22] The appeal of a show like GBBO is that it imagines itself in opposition to this idea of labor and surplus value. If we imagine the contestants as laborers, they seem to exist in a space outside of capitalist time because they produce not for capital, but for pleasure. Baking, after all, so often falls under the provenance of desserts or puddings—that part of the meal that is not about sustenance but about pleasure. Intimacy in this space is predicated on the notion that the contestants bake together without seeking compensation in the traditional sense—there is no prize money. One only takes home a decorative platter and the honor of being Britain's Star Baker. GBBO, by contrast, invites us to slow down and to think of baking as a vocation and not a job. Although many contestants may parlay their success on the show into other successful ventures, they are never valued on the show for producing commodities that can be infinitely reproduced. Rather, it is about slowing down, embracing the process of baking, and creating bonds of intimacy that seemingly run counter to the tenets of the modern nation-state.

Bakers are not alienated from but in proximate intimacy with one another. Indeed, as Josh Freedman notes in an article for *Jacobin*, GBBO is "quietly radical." For Freedman, the lack of financial incentive to compete on the show is a reproach to the very premise of modern capitalism: "In *The Great British*

Bake Off, compassion and sympathy take center stage. Rather than suppress those human impulses, as capitalist competition often encourages, the *Bake Off* allows them to flourish. A failure in the baking tent is not greeted with schadenfreude but with understanding and support."[23]

And yet as Potter and Westall note, shows like GBBO very strategically mine the nation's interest in these purported challenges to late capitalism. They write: "Taking time over shared meals, losing oneself in moments of sensual enjoyment, and savouring episodes of culinary creation or product selection are all exoticised and eroticised even as they are packaged as domestic bliss, culinary care and holistic self-fulfillment. TV chefs have capitalised on the popular uptake of Slow Food's gastronomic localism to depict their own pastoral meanderings into culinary work-for-labour as forms of protection or flight from the urban rush . . . the attractive 'slow' life always relies upon, just as it seeks to escape, a lifestyle built upon professional city-speed and personal wealth."[24]

Baking itself is a particularly interesting case in point. Why is it a show about baking, rather than cooking, that has captured the nation's imagination? Arguably, baking itself as an activity manages time more so than do other forms of cooking. Whereas one can often see the results while cooking and improvise when things go wrong, baking is an investment in a future outcome that one cannot accurately predict until the final product is completed. Baking operates under a different temporality than cooking and requires one to remain optimistic that the ingredients one has assembled will result in a delayed but gratifying payoff.[25]

In their investment in baking as a kind of affective fulfillment, in their investment in the idea that baking together under a white marquee can stave off the pernicious affects of late capitalism, the contestants and viewers of GBBO collectively assent to participate in a willful nostalgia for what will never be. As Lauren Berlant might note, this is a form of cruel optimism insofar as it resolutely focuses on the imagined possibilities of how baking together might lead to a better and more ethical version of the nation. Berlant notes that "a relation of cruel optimism exists when something you desire is actually an obstacle to your flourishing. It might involve food, or a kind of love; it might be a fantasy of the good life, or a political project. It might rest on something simpler, too, like a new habit that promises to induce in you an improved way of being. These kinds of optimistic relation are not inherently cruel. They become cruel only when the object that draws your attachment actively impedes the aim that brought you to it initially."[26]

GBBO, then, relies on viewers' and contestants' ability to access a kind of cruel optimism. After all, what could be more compelling than the idea that if we bake together in a space that is not quite the past but looks very much like what we want the future to be, we can all collectively build a better good life? Intimacy in this context becomes defined by its structural investment in the possibility of a kind of cruel optimism that at once recognizes the false promises of baking together leading to better community while also providing a temporary salve from all the forms of inequality, despair, and lack of hope that make it necessary for these forms of optimism—however cruel—to emerge.

Epilogue

To take a step back and look at the overall argument this book has put forward, the *Great British Bake Off* (*GBBO*) is perhaps instructive in thinking through the pleasures, possibilities, and impossibilities that an intimate eating public can produce for rethinking radical ways to belong and not belong to larger collectives.[1] As the *GBBO* makes clear, intimate eating publics can take various shapes and forms. Now more than ever the white tent and its vision of a possible utopia is awfully seductive and arguably necessary for the imagination. When I started writing this epilogue in March 2020, I was just beginning to practice the self-isolation and social distancing rendered necessary by the coronavirus pandemic, avoiding interactions in public. At the time—only seven days since I had last shared a meal with friends in person and indoors—I had already begun to radically rethink what it means to be part of an intimate eating public, even as I knew that I remained committed to establishing nonnormative and nonromantic ties with friends and chosen family. As the weeks turned into months, I slowly, often begrudgingly, accepted the unexpected pleasures of solo dining while acclimating to the idea that for the foreseeable future most of my meals would be eaten within the space of my loft and that I would not eat in public or semipublic dining spaces with my friends in close physical proximity. We planned to harness synchronous forms of media in order to eat together virtually, while maintaining social distance, during those early months. Underlying all of these plans was a desire to make it possible for intimate eating publics to continue to thrive and flourish, especially for those of us who, in the absence of public spaces in which to gather and in the absence of others within our home spaces, must find alternative ways to broker intimacy with these emergent publics. In the early days of the pandemic, optimism was high that these kinds of intimacies would enable people to curate ways of coming together without being in physical proximity, partly because few of us had a developed sense of how long we would be living under pandemic conditions. And yet it felt inexorably cruel to find moments of fleeting optimism when we did not fully know the *longue durée* of this pandemic. As the days turned into weeks and the weeks into months, that optimism turned to despair. Now, a year later in May 2021, I have managed to find a way to eat outside with friends. I have not eaten inside a restaurant since March 10, 2020, and despite being fully vaccinated, it took quite some time before I felt comfortable enough to sit inside a restaurant again. My initial excitement about getting to hone my culinary skills meant that I have learned to cook all manner of foods: pork vindaloo, gluten-free chickpea flour bread, *gulab jamun*–flavored rice, fresh spring rolls, kalua pork, *jjapaguri*, lamb korma, shiitake mushroom risotto, squash blossom flower quesadillas, nasturtium avocado tacos, *elote*, salted caramel matzo, several types of udon, spam fried rice—the list is endless. But a year later, I have grown tired of this. COVID-19 has taken away the pleasure of solo eating because it is not a respite from the noise of everyday. It *is* my everyday. To eat alone has meant the loss of a kind of intimacy; more importantly, this kind of solo dining has been resolutely placed within the realm of the private, and there is no discernible intimate eating public that can form as easily as it once did when mobility was something we took for granted. I tire of my food. I tire of cooking. I cannot wrap my mind around the terrible *longue durée* of this pandemic. But every few days I snap out of my malaise and try optimistically to embrace the possibility and to remind myself that this is provisional: *It eventually will end.*

The narratives that emerge through each chapter of this book implicitly navigate the multiple ways in which intimate eating publics are formed through provisional spaces—some that feel hopeful and others that feel unrelentingly depressing. And yet eating alone, eating alone together with friends, sharing recipes to cook with limited supplies in the pantry during a time of pandemic are all ways that we are now figuratively in the "white tent" of GBBO together at this moment in 2021.

On September 25, 2020, GBBO returned to US televisions via the streaming service Netflix, with the moniker *The Great British Baking Show*. As noted in the *Los Angeles Times*, the show returned at precisely the moment when baking has hit an all-time high in popularity in the United States. Meredith Blake notes: "In the early months of quarantine, so many people were passing the time by baking—especially bread—that there was a nationwide shortage of yeast (leading, in turn, to a craze for sourdough). Many of us have imagined Paul Hollywood pointing to our sad homemade ciabatta loaves and saying in his Liverpool accent: *'It's undah-prooooooved.'"*[2]

As the first episode of the eighth season begins, the new host Matt Lucas speaks in the characteristically dulcet tones that begin the show. He explains how the bakers have consented to quarantine together for seven weeks; they will live in a "bake off bubble" and thereby create a provisional intimate public with the hosts and their fellow contestants. As Lucas narrates the premise and structure of this COVID-era season, we see a National Health Service–themed cake decorated with masked health-care workers. With an awareness that this show was filmed during the COVID-19 pandemic, it becomes somewhat jarring to see the show enacting normalcy. None of the contestants are wearing face masks or plastic face shields. No partitions separate the participants. They are not social distancing. As Meredith Blake notes: "People stand inches apart, with no plexiglass partitions to be seen, grazing one another's shoulders and elbows with wanton abandon. They even . . . *hug*. And if production assistants are frantically wiping down every piece of equipment in the tent—as they probably are—their efforts do not appear on camera. And, to be honest, the sense of normalcy is a profound relief. The real world is a waking nightmare, but in the tent, it's cake week."[3] Indeed, the eighth season of *GBBO* restores a sense of normalcy for but a fleeting moment in late 2020. For an hour a week for a few months, television viewers are privy to a kind of intimacy that *GBBO* has always espoused but never fully harnessed. For the first time, the contestants and hosts who are part of a "pandemic pod" access a kinship that is not about familial ties but about the familiar, seemingly enacting what has been said so often during the early months of COVID-19: "We are in this together." And so the white tent becomes a space of refuge. It is an alternate imagined intimate public that so forcefully enacts that vision of utopia that so many of us desire as part of our possible future.

For now, cooking continues, eating continues, and different intimacies emerge among strangers. We may access delivery services, drop off meals and hand sanitizer at friends' front doors, eat alone, or engage in other forms of virtual digital intimacy. We may order carryout from Senegalese, Somali, Bhutanese, or Chinese restaurants opened by refugees to make the familiar stranger not feel that their food is suspect. In fact, it is only by imagining the radical possibilities of ways to belong that people who do not fall within the parameters of the couple or the family are able to find hope in an era of social distancing. I am reminded of Sara Ahmed's closing words in *Strange Encounters*, a thoughtful mediation on how we find forms of feminist collectivity through our willingness to engage with strangers. Following Ahmed, I suggest that radical forms of community can be established if we are willing to think outside of the tent, to look to strangers for what we can learn from them, and to insist on accessing the more radical possibilities that eating together may usher in. In other words, we must remake "what it is that we may yet have in common."[4] As I write these words in May 2021, I also try to imagine what the future may bring. Utopic as it may seem, these possibilities that emerge from imagining and bringing to life different social worlds, sustaining and imagining different intimate eating publics, may ultimately be the most radical thing we do during what has felt for so many of us like the most precarious, frightening, and uncertain of times.

Notes

Introduction

1 Elam et al., "Beyond the Face," 139.
2 Elam et al., "Beyond the Face," 139.
3 Elam et al., "Beyond the Face," 140.
4 Elam et al., "Beyond the Face," 140.
5 For further details about this exhibit, including details about the materials used to make the exhibit, see Sita Bhaumik's website, http://www.sitabhaumik.com/the -curry-institute (accessed February 7, 2020).
6 Elam et al., "Beyond the Face," 141.
7 Elam et al., "Beyond the Face," 141.
8 Warner, *Publics and Counterpublics*, 5.
9 For Koichi Iwabuchi, cultural deodorization is a process by which traces of foreign-ness are removed from commodities as they enter a global market. As he notes, "The cultural odor of a product is also closely associated with racial and bodily images of a country of origin." Iwabuchi, *Recentering Globalization*, 128.
10 Sammells and Searles, "Restaurants, Fields, Markets, and Feasts," 129.
11 Sammells and Searles, "Restaurants, Fields, Markets, and Feasts," 130.
12 Sammells and Searles, "Restaurants, Fields, Markets, and Feasts," 130.
13 Erickson, quoted in Sammells and Searles, "Restaurants, Fields, Markets, and Feasts," 130.
14 Bhabha, *Location of Culture*, 37.
15 Gopinath, *Unruly Visions*, 4.
16 For a useful discussion on the role of the stranger and how the immigrant or racially marked body is often deemed to be a stranger who is out of place, see Sara Ahmed's *Strange Encounters*.
17 Berlant, "Intimacy: A Special Issue," 285.

18 Berlant, "Intimacy: A Special Issue," 286.

19 Woodcock, "Narratives of Intimacy," 1044.

20 In large part this idea has been the driving impetus behind the 2020 series *Taste the Nation*, hosted by Padma Lakshmi. As she tours the United States sampling various immigrant and Indigenous cuisines, her show drives home the point that food is complex and helps us to understand the lives of immigrants who make up the nation. The show is not without its detractors. As Bettina Makalintal notes, "The language of 'food unites us,' as it's sold in shows and stories like these, suggests that because we eat similarly, our beliefs must be more similar than we think. Through food, we are all American—or at least, that's the tale these shows want us to believe. But as nice as this idea is—as much as it inspires a wholesome image of a communal American table—who is this narrative meant for, and who does it ultimately serve?" See Makalintal, "Does Food Actually Unite Us?"

21 Camacho, *Migrant Imaginaries*, 4.

22 Hernandez, "Forming Family Identity," 22.

Chapter 1. The Tiffin Box and Gendered Mobility

1 Although Harris uses the spelling *dabbawallah*, several transliterations exist, including *dabbawalla*, *dabbawala*, *dabavala*, and variants thereof. For consistency I use the spelling *dabbawalla* unless the word is spelled otherwise in the source material.

2 Harris, "An Indian Appetizer, Subtly Spiced."

3 Patkar, "In Conversation with: Valay Shende."

4 Krishnamachari, "An Interview with Bose Krishnamachari."

5 Krishnamachari, "An Interview with Bose Krishnamachari."

6 Seen and Gaensheimer, *Subodh Gupta: Everything Is Inside.*

7 For an important and interesting reading about the materials Gupta uses in his art, see Allie Biswas's "Dialectics of the Local and Global in the Work of Subodh Gupta." There, Biswas discusses the historical importance behind each of the natural and human-made materials that Gupta uses. She usefully notes that many of Gupta's installations use stainless steel, a material that is commonplace in Indian home kitchens. And indeed, the dabbas in *Faith Matters* are made of stainless steel and speak to a moment in India's history that saw the ascension of stainless steel as the material of choice for most cooking utensils and eating ware among the Indian middle class.

8 Conlon, "Dining Out in Bombay," 115.

9 Bose Krishnamachari quoted in Mehta, "Think Out of the Dabba."

10 Mehta, "Think Out of the Dabba."

11 Marathi is the main, and official, language of Maharashtra, the state that is home to many of the dabbawallas.

12 The word *tiffin* is used interchangeably with *dabba* and refers to the actual stainless-steel tiered lunchbox. The person who transports the meals is known as a dabbawalla.

13 Ascertaining the actual number of home-cooked meals that are delivered daily is a complicated task. Critical and peer-reviewed studies do not necessarily settle on the same number. One study, for instance, estimates the number of delivered lunches to be about 175,000, whereas another study estimates the number to be 400,000. For the purpose of my argument, the actual number is less relevant than the kinds of narratives that emerge about the labor of the dabbawalla.

14 Conlon, "Dining Out in Bombay," 97.

15 Conlon, "Dining Out in Bombay," 97.

16 Bhattacharya, "Introduction: Mapping Social Reproduction Theory," 15.

17 Ternikar, "Feeding the Muslim South Asian Immigrant Family," 157.

18 Raghunath Medge quoted in Krishnan, "Literacy Practices in Lunch Pails," 176.

19 Pathak, "Delivering the Nation," 251.

20 Pathak, "Delivering the Nation," 239.

21 Balakrishnan and Teo, "Mumbai Tiffin (Dabba) Express," 273.

22 Balakrishnan and Teo, "Mumbai Tiffin (Dabba) Express," 275.

23 Street, Social Literacies, 22.

24 Krishnan, "Literacy Practices in Lunch Pails," 182.

25 Chakrabarty, "Fast Food."

26 Naficy, An Accented Cinema, 101.

27 Naficy, An Accented Cinema, 101.

28 Halberstam, Queer Art of Failure, 11–12.

29 Halberstam, Queer Art of Failure, 3.

30 Altman, Epistolarity: Approaches to a Form, 119.

31 The DVD edition of The Lunchbox comes with a booklet of all the letters exchanged between Ila and Saajan, thereby highlighting the epistolary nature of the film.

32 Rey Chow describes the acousmatic voice, a derivation of Michel Chion's theory of acousmêtre, as a disembodied vocal presence whose presence remains invisible to the viewer. Deshpande Aunty thus is an acousmatic presence insofar as we hear her conversing with Ila, dispensing advice and often sending ingredients down in a basket. But she never appears on screen. See Chow, "The Writing Voice in Cinema."

33 Rahman, "Covert Communications," 492.

34 Mannur, Culinary Fictions, 51.

35 Chow, "The Writing Voice in Cinema," 26–27.

Chapter 2. Cooking for One and the Gustatory Gaze

1 Arendt, "Ideology and Terror," 322.

2 Arendt, "Ideology and Terror," 323.

3 Arendt, "Ideology and Terror," 324.

4 Arendt, "Ideology and Terror," 100.

5 Arendt, "Ideology and Terror," 98.

6 Arendt, "Ideology and Terror," 98–99.

7 Cobb, *Single*, 4.

8 Cobb, *Single*, 21.

9 Gopinath, *Impossible Desires,* 15–16.

10 Rockwell, "Creating Public Intimacy."

11 Claiborne, "Dining Alone," 42.

12 For Claiborne, the "spinster of comfortable means in Manhattan who enjoys dining alone" calls ahead to restaurants to make reservations. She notes that she is visiting from out of town and would the restaurant accommodate a solo female diner. According to Claiborne it is this fact of being from out of town that leads restaurants to make exceptions to policies that typically did not allow women to dine alone.

13 Claiborne, "Dining Alone," 42.

14 Crawford, quoted in Dai, "UES Socialite Restaurant under Fire."

15 Crawford, quoted in Dai, "UES Socialite Restaurant under Fire."

16 Miho Aikawa, "Dinner in NY," accessed June 15, 2020, http://www.mihophoto.com /portfolio/dinnerinny/.

17 Zimmerman, "Women Laughing Alone with Salad."

18 Mani, *Unseeing Empire*, 4.

19 Mani, *Unseeing Empire*, 4.

20 Mani, *Unseeing Empire*, 5.

21 "Padma Lakshmi in Steamy New Ad."

22 Mohanraj, *Bodies in Motion*, 30.

23 Mohanraj, *Bodies in Motion*, 275.

24 Mohanraj, *Bodies in Motion*, 268.

25 Mohanraj, *Bodies in Motion*, 268.

26 Mohanraj, *Bodies in Motion*, 271.

27 Mohanraj, *Bodies in Motion*, 275.

28 Manalansan, "Servicing the World," 218.

29 Mohanraj, *Bodies in Motion*, 272.

30 Mohanraj, *Bodies in Motion*, 269.

31 Mohanraj, *Bodies in Motion*, 273.

32 Detloff, *Persistence of Modernism*, 14–15.

33 Halberstam, *Queer Art of Failure*, 2–3.

34 Mohanraj, *Bodies in Motion*, 271.

35 Daley, "The UK Now Has a 'Minister for Loneliness.'"

36 Thomas Mair "repeatedly shot and stabbed Cox in an attack during the European Union Referendum Campaign in June 2016. While attacking her he said: 'This is for Britain,' 'keep Britain independent,' and 'Britain first,' the court heard." Quoted in Slawson, "Jo Cox Murder Accused Gives Name."

37 Mead, "What Britain's 'Minister of Loneliness' Says."

Chapter 3. Eat, Dwell, Orient

1   Julie Powell, *The Julie/Julia Project* (blog), August 25, 2002, http://blogs.salon.com /0001399/2002/08/25.html.

2   For an extended discussion of how racial formations work within the digital space, see Nakamura, *Digitizing Race.*

3   Lenhart and Fox, "Bloggers: A Portrait of the Internet's New Storytellers."

4   Pham, "Blog Ambition," 7.

5   Andrew Keen, quoted in Pham, "Blog Ambition," 7.

6   In an article about the use of the microblogging social media platform Twitter by gourmet food trucks in New York City, Alison Caldwell argues that Twitter has met with similar criticism. In particular, critiques have been levied as to Twitter being an "irrelevant waste" and space for "pointless messages." See Caldwell, "Will Tweet for Food."

7   One can perhaps deem this function of the blog to be Derridean, in part because the world of food blogging, in the most expansive sense, can allow for a strong counter-narrative to emerge. Because blogs are interested in the supplementary narrative often excised from the printed review, they also provide a space for articulating ideas that might seem tangential but are important to developing a narrative about food. Instead of privileging the master narrative tone of published food reviews that appear in the pages of the *New York Times*, for example, the supplement allows for the idea of authority so central to food reviewing to be decentered.

8   Denveater, "Virtual Roundtable," 45.

9   Trivedi-Grenier's conclusions are part of a larger study exploring how consumers use food blogs and their effects on print journalism. The research, conducted in January 2008, surveyed 1,800 adult food blog readers. Trivedi-Grenier, "New Online Survey Investigates U.S. Food Blog Usage."

10 bell hooks, *Black Looks*, 21.

11 Stacey, "The Global Within," 104.

12 Hage, *White Nation*, 19.

13 "The Plan for Lower Manhattan," accessed July 15, 2011, http://www.renewnyc.com /overlay/ThePlan/.

14 Powell, *Julie & Julia*, 75.

15 Ahmed, *Queer Phenomenology*, 51.

16 The recipe Powell appears to use, from *Mastering the Art of French Cooking*, volume I, is for *bifteck sauté bercy*, a pan-broiled steak with shallot and white wine sauce. A variation of *bifteck sauté au beurre*, the poached beef marrow is an optional addition to the dish.

17 Powell, *Julie & Julia*, 65.

18 Ahmed, *Queer Phenomenology*, 29.

19 Manalansan, "Empire of Food," 94.

20 In the popular television show *Sex and the City*, an episode finds Carrie Bradshaw turning up her nose at an apartment because it smells too much like Indian food. Similarly, a moment from Lauren Weisberger's *Devil Wears Prada* anchors in a culi-

nary register protagonist Andie Sachs's decision to move out of her apartment. See Mannur, *Culinary Fictions*.

21 Powell, *Julie & Julia*, x.

22 Powell, *Julie & Julia*, 14.

23 According to historian Barbara Tuchman (quoted in *Appetite for Life: The Biography of Julia Child*), the South East Asia Command (SEAC) and Office of Strategic Services headquarters were tactically located in Kandy, Sri Lanka, because a fleet base in the Indian Ocean could provide the United States with easy access to the sea in order to launch an attack on Japan. With a high security clearance to file and process for the SEAC classified dispatches concerning US military maneuvering in the Indian Ocean, Child's relationship to place was very much politically oriented toward safeguarding the interests of US imperialism. See Fitch, *Appetite for Life*.

24 Fitch, *Appetite for Life*, 102–3.

25 For more on food pornography and its valences within Asian American Studies, see Wong, *Reading Asian American Literature*; and Xu, *Eating Identities*.

26 I have argued elsewhere that in the late 1990s a familiarity with the easy multiculturalism of fusion cuisine and a willingness to experiment with different culinary styles marked the emergence of a form of cosmopolitan modernity in which, for example, French ingredients easily intermingle with Indian spices. To be a cosmopolitan urban foodie was to be willing to consume difference in the form of the kinds of dishes one might find on the menu of Tabla, Floyd Cardoz's former restaurant, or in the pages of his cookbook, *One Spice, Two Spice*. To be a cosmopolitan foodie was to jettison the excesses of both heavily butter-laden French sauces and overpowering Indian spices in favor of dishes like rawa-crisped skate with rock shrimp and seared striped bass with lime jaggery gastrique. Arguably, such tendency to prefer "lightened" versions of Indian food is also what helped Floyd Cardoz win the title of *Top Chef* Master during cycle 3 of the show. His wild mushroom upma polenta with kokum and coconut milk, notably reworking a common breakfast dish, became a quick favorite for incorporating more sophisticated tastes into the basic dish of upma.

27 In its fetishistic desire to master French cooking while also dreaming of an elsewhere that is not Queens, Powell's rhetoric is eerily reminiscent of that of another avid foodie from the early twentieth century who also sought refuge and comfort amid the textures and tastes of French cuisine. Literary modernist and American exile in Paris Gertrude Stein famously proclaimed about Oakland that there is no there there, and there is something very resonant about the way Julie Powell sees no here in her here—Queens is her Oakland, a space that she cannot imagine being in, and the refuge, not unlike Stein's, is Paris. And, if there can be no living in Queens, there can be no dwelling either.

28 Powell, *Julie & Julia*, 293.

29 Power, *Ginger and Ganesh*, 1.

30 Nakamura, *Digitizing Race*, 173.

31 Power, *Ginger and Ganesh*, 1.

32 Power, *Ginger and Ganesh*, 7.

33 Power, *Ginger and Ganesh*, 5.

34 See Maira, *Desis in the House*; and Prashad, *Karma of Brown Folk*.

35 Pohlhaus, "Relational Knowing and Epistemic Injustice," 731.

36 For example, see Deloria, *Playing Indian*, for a capacious analysis of what it means to play at being Indian. Deloria's example draws from the cultural denigration of Native Americans that was tethered to forms of white supremacy and nationalism, but it is the phrase *playing Indian* that merits further scrutiny. Power's use of the term seems willfully ignorant of this historical and continuing form of anti-Indigenous racism.

37 Although Power's book was published in 2011, Craigslist discontinued its Personals and Casual Encounters sections in 2010. For many, this feature of Craigslist was a means of facilitating forms of stranger intimacy of a more risqué or sexual nature than the kind of stranger intimacy Power seeks out.

38 I thank Sue J. Kim for helping me think about the theoretical nuance of this point.

39 Ahmed, *Strange Encounters*, 113.

40 See Spigel, *Welcome to the Dreamhouse*, for an in-depth discussion of race, whiteness, and suburbanization.

41 See Mitra Kalita, *Suburban Sahibs*; and Tongson, *Relocations*.

42 Tongson, *Relocations*, 36.

43 See Li, *Ethnoburb*.

44 Power, *Ginger and Ganesh*, 6.

45 Williams, "Eat, Pray, Love."

46 Appadurai, *Modernity at Large*, 33.

47 I am referring here to the popular book *The Help*, which was subsequently turned into a film.

48 One can cite many examples of nineteenth-century American and British women's travel narratives as predecessors to Powell's and Power's texts. The general genre of travel narrative in nineteenth-century US literature often features women's (real or imaginary) escape from the restrictions of domesticity (and the illness caused by it) into nature. For example, Kate Chopin's narrative that presents travel to Latin America as an escape from a stifling marriage, Mary Austin's writing about the Native Americans of the US Southwest, and Mary Rowlandson's classic narrative of captivity during colonial America all exemplify this particular trend of fomenting a sense of subjectivity against the subjectivity of the woman of color. Indeed, the trope of rescue and disciplining of racial difference can also be understood to be a way of finding oneself. Within the British literary canon, the writings of Flora Annie Steel and Mary Kingsley are among those that deploy the figure of the woman of color as a foil against which to articulate white female subjectivity.

49 Heidegger, "Building Dwelling Thinking," 145.

50 Karnasiewicz, "Recipe for Success."

51 Highmore, "Out of the Strong Came Forth Sweetness," 17.

52 Damon Scott, email message to the author, September 30, 2011.

53 Dai, *The Lawrence/Julie and Julia Project* (blog), accessed July 20, 2014, http://www.lawrenceandjulieandjulia.com/.

54 One might also remark here on the convergence between Dai's project and Monique Truong's *Book of Salt*. The latter is a fictionalized account of Thin Binh, the Vietnamese cook who worked for Gertrude Stein and Alice B. Toklas in their Paris home. In its work of reimagining the texture of the Steins' Parisian life by recovering the voice of their Vietnamese cook, Truong's work disturbs the seamless whiteness of Stein's Paris or modernist fiction projects, much as Dai's attention to Julia Child disturbs her imagined whiteness as anchored in her penchant for French cuisine.

55 See Eng, *Racial Castration*. In particular, Eng's final chapter, "Out Here and Over There," offers a capacious understanding of how to think through the myriad significations of the hyphen and the cultural and political work it does.

56 Palumbo-Liu, *Asian/American*, 1.

Chapter 4. Tasting Conflict

1 Holden, "Man in the Kitchen Is Hungry for Love."

2 "Eat St.," Cooking Channel, accessed August 21, 2019, https://www.cookingchanneltv .com/shows/eat-st.

3 In this chapter I take Arellano's lead and use the term *lonchera* to describe food trucks, while *lonchero* refers to the cooks who make food in the trucks (loncheras). It is worth noting that other articles cited in this chapter may use the word *lonchera* to describe the food trucks.

4 Arellano, "Where Are the Loncheras at the Luxe-Lonchera Fests?"

5 Furdyk, "Fun with Food: 18 Clever Food Truck Names."

6 Gold, "Moveable Feasts."

7 For an analysis of the emergence of Kogi, see Wang, "Learning from Los Kogi Angeles." In the same volume, also refer to Siu, "Twenty-First-Century Food Trucks." Also see Ku, "'Is That Kimchi in My Taco?'"

8 Hernandez-Lopez, "LA's Taco Truck War," 233.

9 Hernandez-Lopez, "LA's Taco Truck War," 238.

10 Orwell, *Road to Wigan Pier*, 115–16.

11 Knowles has been performing *Make a Salad* for almost six decades. Debuting in 1962 as part of the Fluxus art movement, the large audience-involved performances and installations have been celebrated for the ways in which art allows audiences to collectively create something (in this case a salad) and then to share in the communal experience of eating the prepared dish. See Morais, "Salad as Performance Art."

12 "Feast: Radical Hospitality in Contemporary Art," Smart Museum of Art, University of Chicago, accessed October 1, 2019, https://smartmuseum.uchicago.edu /exhibitions/feast/.

13 Shohat, "Culinary Ghosting."

14 Ahmed, *Strange Encounters*, 97.

15 Ahmed, *Strange Encounters*, 97.

16 Derrida, *Politics of Friendship*, 150.

17 Park, *Cold War Friendships*, 10.

18 Bhaumik, "Edible Text," 73.

19 Bhaumik, "Edible Text," 73.

20 Shohat, "Culinary Ghosting," 220.

21 Although beyond the scope of this chapter, another art installation project inspired by the model of social sculpture is *War Gastronomy: Recipes of Relocation*, a mobile bicycle-based food cart developed by Justin Hoover and Chris Treggiari. The art project is described as follows: "Touched by his Chinese grandmother's tales of escaping war, and by her traditional cooking, Hoover started to collect recipes from people who have been forced to move due to conflict in their home countries. At predetermined times in public places, the pair sets up their cart and serves dishes along with the personal stories attached to them." "War Gastronomy: Recipes of Relocation," *SpontaneousInterventions*, 2012, accessed December 14, 2017, http://www.spontaneousinterventions.org/project/war-gastronomy-recipes-of-relocation/.

22 Beuys, "Beuys Hyperessay."

23 Ngai, "Theory of the Gimmick."

24 Michael Rakowitz, quoted in Glatz, "Weapons of Mass Deliciousness."

25 Julier, *Eating Together*, 6.

26 Ko, "Sweet and Bitter Road."

27 Rakowitz, *Backstroke of the West*, 64.

28 Rakowitz, *Backstroke of the West*, 64.

29 Bhaumik, "Edible Text," 69.

30 Nguyen, *Gift of Freedom*, 6–8.

31 Michael Rakowitz, quoted in Friedman, "Eating Off Saddam's Plates."

32 Bhaumik, "Edible Text," 74.

33 Bhaumik, "Edible Text," 83.

34 See Caldwell, "Will Tweet for Food" for an exploration of the role of social media in building customer bases for food trucks and other mobile eateries.

35 A trip to Cuba to research the foods there led to an impromptu visit to the North Korean mission, which led to imagining possibilities in order to create a context for North Korean cuisine in North America, a point that is notable because Korean food is primarily South Korean and largely unattended to in the culinary imaginary of the US.

36 The menu of each of the rotating iterations of Conflict Kitchen can be found archived on the restaurant's website. See https://www.conflictkitchen.org/about/# (accessed June 23, 2020).

37 Conflict Kitchen, "About," https://www.conflictkitchen.org/about/ (accessed May 7, 2021).

38 Jon Rubin, quoted in Sohmer, "Conflict Kitchen."

39 "Conflict Kitchen," https://www.conflictkitchen.org/ (accessed July 15, 2015).

40 Shah, "Culinary Diplomacy at the Axis of Evil Cafe."

41 Dawn Weleski, quoted in Shah, "Culinary Diplomacy at the Axis of Evil Cafe."

42 Established in 2005, the Anyang Public Art Project (APAP) largely focuses on creat-

ing temporary art installations within the city. Showcasing diverse genres from art to architecture, cinema, and performance, APAP has created space for renowned Korean and international artists including Yayoi Kusama and Rirkrit Tiravanija, among others, to create temporary art installations. They have also partnered with other organizations to do virtual events such as the "North Korean Cooking Lesson." See the organization's website at http://www.apap.or.kr/eng/index.asp.

43 "North Korean Cooking Lesson," http://conflictkitchen.org/events/the-north-korean -cooking-lesson/ (accessed October 1, 2019).

44 As Junaid Rana notes, "each day seems to bring new failure; like Sisyphus, he must start each morning by rolling out his pushcart and earn the money to finally redeem himself." *Terrifying Muslims*, 174–75.

45 Rana, *Terrifying Muslims*, 174.

46 Rana, *Terrifying Muslims*, 175.

47 Caldwell, "Will Tweet for Food," 307. Also see Caldwell's essay for a succinct history of the ways in which street food vending, a fixture in New York City, has dramatically altered since its humble beginnings in the late nineteenth century. Although the luxe lonchera has made its presence felt in New York, street food largely remains the business of first-generation immigrants, often those with lower skills who enter into the food vending business because of its limited capital risk.

48 Bhaumik, "Edible Text," 73.

49 The scholar and podcast host Sam Chapple-Sokol defines *culinary diplomacy* as "the use of food and cuisine as an instrument to create cross-cultural understanding in the hopes of improving interactions and cooperation" (Chapple-Sokol, "Culinary Diplomacy," 161). Offering a perspective that emerges from diplomacy studies, Chapple-Sokol outlines various programs that have been enacted at the state level that are aimed at fostering unity across nations. In a larger sense, the tenets of culinary diplomacy have been enacted as forms of soft power by the governments of at least two Asian nations. In 2002–3 the Thai government launched "Global Thai" and "Kitchen of the World" programs, aimed at increasing the number of Thai restaurants throughout the world. In 2009 the South Korean government launched "Korean Cuisine in the World," a program aimed at making Korean food among the most popular ethnic cuisines in the world. Referred to as "Kimchi Diplomacy," this program—not unlike the undertaking by the government of Thailand—works in tandem with more direct forms of economic power and traditional forms of diplomacy to "put their imprint on the world around them" (174). For more on culinary diplomacy, see the archives of Chapple-Sokol's podcast "Culinary Citizen" at http:// culinarydiplomacy.com/podcasts/. For a comprehensive and more in-depth analysis of the Thai government's undertaking of culinary diplomacy, see Mark Padoong-patt's *Flavors of Empire: Food and the Making of Thai America*. For a discussion of South Korea's use of culinary diplomacy, see Mary Jo A. Pham's "Food as Communication: A Case Study of South Korea's Gastrodiplomacy."

50 Michelle Obama's Let's Move! campaign was not wholly unproblematic. Despite its emphasis on food justice and sustainability, a large and often uncritical discussion of

obesity reproduced ableist ideologies and overlooked the extent to which narratives of fitness simultaneously colluded with ableist understandings of the body that had little to do with actual health. As Theresa Kulbaga and Leland Spencer note, despite its best intentions, the deep focus on fitness implicitly linked "good citizenship with gender, race and able-bodied privilege." Kulbaga and Spencer, "Fitness and the Feminist First Lady," 37.

51 "Diplomatic Culinary Partnership," James Beard Foundation, accessed June 6, 2020, https://www.jamesbeard.org/dcp/.

52 Capricia Penavic Marshall quoted in "Diplomatic Culinary Partnership," James Beard Foundation, accessed June 6, 2020, https://www.jamesbeard.org/dcp/.

Chapter 5. Baking and the Intimate Eating Public

1 Shamsie, *Home Fire.*

2 Please note that although US-based Netflix refers to the show as *The Great British Baking Show*, I refer to the program by its British name, *The Great British Bake Off* because the contexts I am describing have less to do with the forms of viewership in the US and more to do with the construction of intimacy in the British context.

3 Shamsie, *Home Fire.*

4 Anderson, *Imagined Communities*, 7.

5 Anderson, *Imagined Communities*, 6.

6 Shamsie, *Home Fire.*

7 Peri Bradley, for instance, suggests that GBBO presents "a specific positioning of class and class values whose relationship is deeply involved with not only the material substance of food itself, but also its capacity to convey a complex and multicultural British identity that raises questions about the protectionist agenda and ideology of current political policies in the U.K." Bradley, "More Cake Please—We're British!," 10.

8 The *Great British Bake Off* has had a long and storied history in its eight seasons. A creation of Love Productions, the show's first seven seasons featured judges Paul Hollywood and Mary Berry at the helm and with comedians Mel Giedroyc and Sue Perkins serving as the hosts. While the show was initially aired on BBC, its unanticipated success led Love Productions to seek moving the show to the more lucrative Channel Four. In response, Giedroyc, Perkins, and Berry all left the show and were replaced by Noel Fielding and Sandi Toksvig, with Prue Leith replacing the apparently irreplaceable Mary Berry.

9 The context of Brexit and the Windrush Scandal are important to note. In 2018, a controversial political scandal emerged in Britain in which several people of Caribbean ancestry were wrongly detained, deprived of legal rights, and threatened with deportation. According to the *Guardian*, at least eighty-three individuals were wrongly deported by the UK Home Office. The *Windrush Generation* refers to British subjects who migrated to the UK in the late 1940s and 1950s; the first group of these immigrants arrived via the HMT *Empire Windrush* from the West Indies in 1948.

Other members of the Windrush Generation include subjects born in Britain and individuals who had arrived in the UK before 1973. The Windrush Scandal, which occurred at the same time as Britain was moving toward exiting the European Community, is an instantiation of a growing xenophobia in Britain and of wider concerns about British immigration policy and the practices of the Home Office.

10 I borrow the term *coziness* from Erica Maria Cheung, who has described *GBBO* as producing a form of "postcolonial cozy." See Cheung, "Postcolonial Cozy."

11 A comprehensive overview of the dynamics of cooking shows and the motivations of contestants who take part in them can be found in Tasha Oren's excellent article, "On the Line."

12 A case in point of the imagined horizontal comradery that structures the show can be understood if we think about the fracas surrounding the purported sabotage of a baked Alaska on season 5. In the episode, one of the contestants, Diana Beard, allegedly took fellow contestant Iain Watters's ice cream and sponge cake out of the freezer to make room for hers. In the process, she inadvertently left the confection on a counter, where it melted owing to high temperatures inside the baking tent. When Watters discovered the melting confection, he infamously threw the cake into the trash can and was left with nothing to present the judges, thus leading to his elimination. "Bingate," as the episode has been referred to, has been framed as one of the few anomalous moments on the show when less-than-savory motives and unhealthy competition were ascribed to the contestants, despite protestations from many that Beard's action was a genuine mistake and not a deliberate act of sabotage.

13 Although it is common practice in the UK to refer to television seasons as "series," I use the US term *season*. Moreover, I refer to the various seasons in the order in which they were aired and released in the UK and not the US. Several seasons of the show have aired on PBS in the US but not in the order they were released in the UK. At the time of writing, all but the first two seasons of *GBBO* are available via streaming services or exclusively on Netflix in the US.

14 Clark, "'The Great British Bake Off' Changes the Way the British Bake."

15 Bradley, "More Cake Please—We're British!," 19.

16 In his *Principles of Political Economy*, John Stuart Mill (discussed more fully in Edward Said's *Culture and Imperialism*) articulates the extent to which British colonial possessions in the Caribbean are enfolded into the vision of the nation precisely because they provide commodities that are imagined to be enabled by English capital and for consumption among the inhabitants of England. He writes, "These [outlying possessions of ours] are hardly to be looked upon as countries, carrying on an exchange of commodities . . . but more properly as outlying agricultural or manufacturing estates belonging to a larger community. Our West India colonies, for example, cannot be regarded as countries with a productive capital of their own. . . . The West Indies in like manner is the place where England finds it convenient to carry on the production of sugar, coffee and a few other tropical commodities. All the capital employed is English . . . these [staple commodities] are sold in England for the benefit of the proprietors there." Quoted in Said, *Culture and Imperialism*, 94.

17 Said, *Culture and Imperialism*, 94.

18 Said, *Culture and Imperialism*, 96.

19 Varagur, "The Great Brexit Bake Off."

20 Lagerwey, *"The Great British Bake Off,"* 443.

21 Potter and Westall, "Neoliberal Britain's Austerity Foodscape," 161.

22 Marx, *Capital*, 444.

23 Freedman, "The Great Socialist Bake Off."

24 Potter and Westall, "Neoliberal Britain's Austerity Foodscape," 169.

25 I am grateful to Tim August for making this point so eloquently and for sharing this particular insight with me.

26 Berlant, *Cruel Optimism*, 1.

Epilogue

1 As I finish this book, the COVID-19 pandemic has kept us sequestered from one another for more than a year. During the period of "lockdown" in mid-2020, on various social media platforms, people posted pictures and stories revealing how they turned to baking. Although initially framed as a response to limited ingredients available in stores, another narrative also emerged about why people were baking. The act of baking is being described as a form of therapy—whether as stress baking, "procrasti-baking," anxiety baking, or rage baking—to counter the feelings of deep anxiety felt by people who are stuck at home. Weinberg, "Baking Is the Best Way to Alleviate Stress—Yes, Really."

2 Meredith Blake, "'Great British Baking Show' Is the COVID-Free TV Comfort Food We Need Right Now," *Los Angeles Times*, September 25, 2020, accessed September 28, 2020, https: //www.latimes.com/entertainment-arts/tv/story/2020-09-25/great-british-bake-off-netflix-covid-pandemic.

3 Blake, "'Great British Baking Show' Is the COVID-Free TV Comfort Food We Need Right Now."

4 Ahmed, *Strange Encounters*, 181.

Works Cited

Ahmed, Sara. *Queer Phenomenology: Orientations, Objects, Others.* Durham, NC: Duke University Press, 2005.

Ahmed, Sara. *Strange Encounters: Embodied Others in Post-Coloniality.* London: Routledge, 2000.

Aikawa, Miho. "Miho Aikawa Photography." Accessed September 12, 2020. http://www.mihophoto.com.

Altman, Janet Gurkin. *Epistolarity: Approaches to a Form.* New Haven, CT: Yale University Press, 1973.

Anderson, Benedict. *Imagined Communities: Reflections on the Origin and Spread of Nationalism.* London: Verso, 2016.

Appadurai, Arjun. *Modernity at Large: Cultural Dimensions of Globalization.* Minneapolis: University of Minnesota Press, 1996.

Arellano, Gustavo. "Where Are the Loncheras at the Luxe-Lonchera Fests?" *OC Weekly* (blog), September 2, 2010. Accessed August 21, 2019. https://www.ocweekly.com/where-are-the-loncheras-at-the-luxe-lonchera-fests-6617846/?sfw=pass1616762937.

Arendt, Hannah. "Ideology and Terror: A Novel Form of Government." *Review of Politics* 15, no. 3 (July 1953): 303–32.

Arendt, Hannah. *The Origins of Totalitarianism.* New York: Harcourt and Brace, 1951.

Bahrani, Ramin, dir. *Man Push Cart.* DVD. Port Washington, NY: Koch Lorber Films, 2005.

Bailey, Timothy, and Mike B. Anderson, dirs. *The Simpsons.* Season 23, episode 5, "The Food Wife." Aired November 13, 2011, on FOX.

Balakrishnan, Natarajan, and Chung-Piaw Teo. "Mumbai Tiffin (Dabba) Express." In *Supply Chain Analysis: A Handbook on the Interaction of Information, System and Optimization,* edited by Christopher Tang, Chung-Piaw Teo, and Kwok-Kei Wei, 272–78. Palo Alto, CA: Fred Hillier, 2008.

Batra, Ritesh, dir. *The Lunchbox*. DVD. New York: Sony Pictures Classic, 2014.

Berlant, Lauren. *Cruel Optimism*. Durham, NC: Duke University Press, 2011.

Berlant, Lauren. "Intimacy: A Special Issue." *Critical Inquiry* 24, no. 2 (1998): 281–88.

Beuys, Joseph. "Beuys Hyperessay." Walker Art Center. Accessed September 15, 2013. http://www.walkerart.org/archive/8/A44369ADE26CA3996178.htm. Site no longer available.

Bhabha, Homi. *The Location of Culture*. London: Routledge, 2004.

Bhattacharya, Tithi. "Introduction: Mapping Social Reproduction Theory." In *Social Reproduction Theory: Remapping Class, Recentering Oppression*, 1–20. London: Pluto Press, 2017.

Bhaumik, Sita Kuratomi. "Eating the Enemy: Edible Strategies in Enemy Kitchen and Prison Gourmet." In *Multiple Elementary*, edited by Helen Reed and Hannah Jickling, 38–51. Toronto: YYZ Books, 2017.

Bhaumik, Sita Kuratomi. "The Edible Text: Representational Strategies in the Art of Michael Rakowitz." *Sightlines* (2012): 63–85.

Biswas, Allie. "Dialectics of the Local and Global in the Work of Subodh Gupta." In *Dislocating Globality: Deterritorialization, Difference and Resistance*, edited by Šarūnas Paunksnis, 47–76. Leiden: Brill, 2015.

Bradley, Peri. "More Cake Please—We're British! Locating British Identity in Contemporary TV Food Texts, *The Great British Bake Off* and *Come Dine with Me*." In *Food, Media and Contemporary Culture: The Edible Image*, edited by Peri Bradley, 9–26. London: Palgrave Macmillan, 2016.

Caldwell, Alison. "Will Tweet for Food: Microblogging Mobile Food Trucks—Online, Offline, and In Line." In *Taking Food Public: Redefining Foodways in a Changing World*, edited by Psyche Williams-Forson and Carole Counihan, 306–21. London: Routledge, 2011.

Cardoz, Floyd. *One Spice, Two Spice: American Food, Indian Flavors*. New York: William Morrow, 2006.

Chakrabarty, Subrata. "Fast Food." *Forbes*, August 9, 1998. Accessed June 23, 2020. http://www.forbes.com/global/1998/0810/0109078a.html.

Chapple-Sokol, Sam. "Culinary Diplomacy: Breaking Bread to Win Hearts and Minds." *The Hague Journal of Diplomacy* 8 (2013): 161–83.

Cheung, Erica Maria. "Postcolonial Cozy." In Media Res: A MediaCommons Project, February 15, 2017. Accessed March 27, 2020. http://mediacommons.org/imr/2017/02/15/postcolonial-cozy.

Chin, Frank. *The Chickencoop Chinaman and The Year of the Dragon: Two Plays*. Seattle: University of Washington Press, 1981.

Chow, Rey. "The Writing Voice in Cinema: A Preliminary Discussion." In *Locating the Voice in Film: Critical Approaches and Global Practices*, edited by Tom Whittaker and Sarah Wright, 17–30. Oxford: Oxford University Press, 2017.

Claiborne, Craig. "Dining Alone Can Pose Problem for a Woman." *New York Times*, June 16, 1964, 42.

Clark, Melissa. "'The Great British Bake Off' Changes the Way the British Bake." *New*

York Times, October 18, 2016. https://www.nytimes.com/2016/10/19/dining/great
-british-bake-off-recipes.html.

Cobb, Michael. *Single: Arguments for the Uncoupled*. New York: New York University Press, 2012. Kindle.

Conlon, Frank. "Dining Out in Bombay." In *Consuming Modernity: Public Culture in a South Asian World*, edited by Carol Breckenridge, 90–127. Minneapolis: University of Minnesota Press, 1995.

Dai, Lawrence. "Day 31—Racism in Julie and Julia (pt. 1)." *The Lawrence/Julie and Julia Project* (blog), December 30, 2010. Accessed October 1, 2011. http://www.lawrence andjulieandjulia.com/.

Dai, Serena. "UES Socialite Restaurant under Fire for Allegedly Banning a Solo Female Diner at the Bar." *Eater New York*, January 18, 2019. Accessed June 15, 2020. https:// ny.eater.com/2019/1/18/18188454/nello-upper-east-side-solo-diner-bar-female.

Daley, Jason. "The UK Now Has a 'Minister for Loneliness.' Here's Why It Matters." *Smithsonian Magazine*, January 19, 2018. Accessed September 11, 2020. https:// www.smithsonianmag.com/smart-news/minister-loneliness-appointed-united -kingdom-180967883/.

Deloria, Philip. *Playing Indian*. New Haven, CT: Yale University Press, 1999.

Denveater. "The Virtual Roundtable: Food Blogging as Citizen Journalism." *World Literature Today* 83, no. 1 (2009): 42–45.

Derrida, Jacques. *The Politics of Friendship*. Translated by George Collins. London: Verso, 2005.

Derrida, Jacques. *The Post Card: From Socrates to Freud and Beyond*. Translated by Alan Bass. Chicago: University of Chicago Press, 1987.

Detloff, Madelyn. *The Persistence of Modernism: Loss and Mourning in the Twentieth Century*. Cambridge: Cambridge University Press, 2009.

"The Diplomatic Culinary Partnership." James Beard Foundation. Accessed June 6, 2020. https://www.jamesbeard.org/dcp.

Elam, Michele, Laura Kina, Jeff Chang, and Ellen Oh. "Beyond the Face: A Pedagogical Primer for Mixed-Race Art and Social Engagement." *Asian American Literary Review*, no. 2 (fall 2013): 120–54.

Eng, David L. *Racial Castration: Managing Masculinity in Asian America*. Durham, NC: Duke University Press, 2001.

Fitch, Noel Riley. *Appetite for Life: The Biography of Julia Child*. New York: Anchor, 1999.

Freedman, Josh. "The Great Socialist Bake Off." *Jacobin Magazine*. Accessed September 12, 2020. https://www.jacobinmag.com/2019/09/great-british-bake-off-baking -show-socialism.

Friedman, Uri. "Eating Off Saddam's Plates: Iraqi Militaria as a Hobby." *The Atlantic*, October 14, 2011. Accessed June 22, 2020. https://www.theatlantic.com/international /archive/2011/10/eating-saddams-plates-iraqi-militaria-hobby/336734/.

Furdyk, Brent. "Fun with Food: 18 Clever Food Truck Names." Food Network. Accessed August 21, 2019. https://www.foodnetwork.ca/fun-with-food/photos/clever-funny -food-truck-names/. Site no longer available.

Gilbert, Elizabeth. *Eat, Pray, Love: One Woman's Search for Everything across Italy, India and Indonesia*. New York: Riverhead Books, 2006.

Glatz, Julianne. "Weapons of Mass Deliciousness." *Illinois Times*, May 17, 2012. Accessed September 12, 2020. https://www.illinoistimes.com/springfield/weapons-of-mass -deliciousness/Content?oid=11443984.

Gold, Jonathan. "Moveable Feasts." *Smithsonian Magazine* 42, no. 11 (2012): 18–19.

Gopinath, Gayatri. *Impossible Desires: Queer Diasporas and South Asian Public Cultures*. Durham, NC: Duke University Press, 2005.

Gopinath, Gayatri. *Unruly Visions: The Aesthetic Practices of Queer Diaspora*. Durham, NC: Duke University Press, 2018.

The Great British Baking Show. Collection 6, episode 9, "Vegan Week." Aired October 9, 2018, on Netflix. https://www.netflix.com/watch/81001560?trackId=14277283 &tctx=-97%2C-97%2C%2C%2C%2C.

Hage, Ghassan. *White Nation: Fantasies of White Supremacy in a Multicultural Society*. New York: Routledge, 2000.

Halberstam, Jack. *The Queer Art of Failure*. Durham, NC: Duke University Press, 2011.

Hall, Stuart. "Old and New Identities, Old and New Ethnicities." In *Culture, Globalization, and the World-System: Contemporary Conditions for the Representation of Identity*, edited by Anthony D. King, 41–68. Minneapolis: University of Minnesota Press, 1997.

Harris, Gardiner. "An Indian Appetizer, Subtly Spiced." *New York Times*, February 21, 2014. Accessed June 24, 2020. https://www.nytimes.com/2014/02/23/movies /the-lunchbox-a-bollywood-anomaly-comes-to-america.html.

Heidegger, Martin. "Building Dwelling Thinking." In *Poetry, Language, Thought*, translated by Albert Hofstadter, 141–59. New York: Harper Colophon, 1971.

Hernandez, Michael. "Forming Family Identity in an American Chinese Restaurant: One Person's Transformational Process." In *The Restaurants Book: Ethnographies of Where We Eat*, edited by David Beriss and David Sutton, 25–34. Oxford: Berg, 2007.

Hernandez-Lopez, Ernesto. "LA's Taco Truck War: How Law Cooks Food Culture Contests." *University of Miami Inter-American Law Review* 43, no. 1 (2011): 233–68.

Highmore, Ben. "Out of the Strong Came Forth Sweetness—Sugar on the Move." *New Formations* 74 (2011): 5–17.

Holden, Stephen. "Man in the Kitchen Is Hungry for Love." *New York Times*, May 8, 2014. Accessed August 21, 2019. https://www.nytimes.com/2014/05/09/movies/chef -a-culinary-comedy-by-jon-favreau.html.

hooks, bell. *Black Looks: Race and Representation*. London: Turnaround, 1992.

Iwabuchi, Koichi. *Recentering Globalization: Popular Culture and Japanese Transnationalism*. Durham, NC: Duke University Press, 2002.

Julier, Alice P. *Eating Together: Food, Friendship, and Inequality*. Urbana: University of Illinois Press, 2013.

Karnasiewicz, Sarah. "Recipe for Success." Salon.com, October 12, 2005. Accessed September 15, 2020. https://www.salon.com/2005/10/12/powell_27/.

Kauffman, Linda. *Special Delivery: Epistolary Modes in Modern Fiction*. Chicago: University of Chicago Press, 1992.

Kerman, Piper. *Orange Is the New Black: My Year in a Women's Prison*. New York: Random House, 2011.

Kingsolver, Barbara, Camille Kingsolver, and Steven Hopp. *Animal, Vegetable, Miracle: A Year of Food Life*. New York: HarperCollins, 2008.

Kini, Abhijeet. *Dabbawala: Feeding Mumbai since 1890*. Mumbai: SodaBottleOpenerWala, 2019.

Ko, Hanae. "The Sweet and Bitter Road." *ArtAsiaPacific* 78 (2012). Accessed September 18, 2020. http://artasiapacific.com/Magazine/78/TheSweetAndBitterRoad MichaelRakowitz.

Krishnamachari, Bose. "An Interview with Bose Krishnamachari." Accessed June 24, 2020. http://www.theartstrust.com/Magazine_article.aspx?articleid=18. Site no longer available.

Krishnan, Uma. "Literacy Practices in Lunch Pails: Invisible Literacies of the Dabbawalas." In *Literacy in Practice: Writing in Private, Public, and Working Lives*, edited by Patrick Thomas and Pamela Takayoshi, 176–88. New York: Routledge, 2016.

Ku, Robert Ji-Song. "'Is That Kimchi in My Taco?' A Vision of Korean American Food in One Bite." In *A Companion to Korean American Studies*, edited by Rachael Miyung Joo and Shelley Sang-Hee Lee, 128–49. Leiden: Brill, 2018.

Ku, Robert Ji-Song, Martin F. Manalansan IV, and Anita Mannur, eds. *Eating Asian America: A Food Studies Reader*. New York: New York University Press, 2013.

Kulbaga, Theresa, and Leland Spencer. "Fitness and the Feminist First Lady: Gender, Race, and Body in Michelle Obama's Let's Move! Campaign." *Women and Language* 40, no. 1 (2018): 36–48.

Lagerwey, Jorie. "*The Great British Bake Off*, Joy, and the Affective Potential of Nadiya Hussain's Amateur Celebrity." *Celebrity Studies* 9, no. 4 (2018): 442–54.

Lenhart, Amanda, and Susannah Fox. "Bloggers: A Portrait of the Internet's New Storytellers." Pew Internet and American Life Project. Accessed October 15, 2011. http://www.pewinternet.org/Reports/2006/Bloggers.aspx. Site no longer available.

Li, Wei. *Ethnoburb: The New Ethnic Community in Urban America*. Honolulu: University of Hawai'i Press, 2009.

Maira, Sunaina. *Desis in the House: Indian American Youth Culture in New York City*. Philadelphia: Temple University Press, 2002.

Makalintal, Bettina. "Does Food Actually Unite Us?" *Vice*, June 29, 2020. Accessed June 30, 2020. https://www.vice.com/en_us/article/xg8gvk/does-food-actually-unite-us.

Manalansan, Martin F., IV. "The Empire of Food: Place, Memory, and Asian 'Ethnic Cuisines.'" In *Gastropolis: Food and New York City*, edited by Annie Hauck-Lawson and Jonathan Deutsch, 93–107. New York: Columbia University Press, 2008.

Manalansan, Martin F., IV. "Immigrant Lives and the Politics of Olfaction in the Global City." In *The Smell Culture Reader*, edited by Jim Drobnick, 41–52. Oxford: Berg, 2006.

Manalansan, Martin F., IV. "Servicing the World: Flexible Filipinos and the Unsecured

Life." In *Political Emotions*, edited by Janet Staiger, Ann Cvetkovich, and Ann Reynolds, 215–28. New York: Taylor and Francis, 2010.

Mani, Bakirathi. *Unseeing Empire: Photography, Representation, South Asian America*. Durham, NC: Duke University Press, 2020.

Mannur, Anita. *Culinary Fictions: Food in South Asian Diasporic Culture*. Philadelphia: Temple University Press, 2010.

Marx, Karl. *Capital: A Critical Analysis of Capitalist Production London*. Berlin: Dietz Verlag, [1887] 1990.

Mead, Rebecca. "What Britain's 'Minister of Loneliness' Says about Brexit and the Legacy of Jo Cox." *New Yorker*, January 26, 2018. Accessed June 15, 2020. https://www.newyorker.com/culture/cultural-comment/britain-minister-of-loneliness-brexit-jo-cox.

Mehta, Mithila. "Think Out of the Dabba." *Mumbai Mirror*, updated February 25, 2008. http://www.mumbaimirror.com/others/sunday-read/Think-out-of-the-Dabba/articleshow/15789030.cms.

Mill, John Stuart. *Principles of Political Economy with Some of Their Applications to Social Philosophy*. Edited by W. J. Ashley. London: Longmans, Green and Co., 1909.

Mitra Kalita, S. *Suburban Sahibs: Three Immigrant Families and Their Passage from India to America*. New Brunswick, NJ: Rutgers University Press, 2005.

Mohanraj, Mary Anne. *Bodies in Motion*. New York: HarperCollins, 2006.

Morais, Betsy. "Salad as Performance Art." *New Yorker*, April 26, 2012. Accessed September 18, 2020. https://www.newyorker.com/culture/culture-desk/salad-as-performance-art.

Naficy, Hamid. *An Accented Cinema: Exilic and Diasporic Filmmaking*. Princeton, NJ: Princeton University Press, 2001.

Nakamura, Lisa. *Digitizing Race: Visual Cultures of the Internet*. Minneapolis: University of Minnesota Press, 2008.

Ngai, Sianne. "Theory of the Gimmick." *Critical Inquiry* 43 (2017): 466–505.

Nguyen, Mimi Thi. *The Gift of Freedom: War, Debt, and Other Refugee Passages*. Durham, NC: Duke University Press, 2012.

"The North Korean Cooking Lesson." *Conflict Kitchen*, December 6, 2013. Accessed October 1, 2019. http://conflictkitchen.org/events/the-north-korean-cooking-lesson/.

Oren, Tasha. "On the Line: Format, Cooking and Competition as Television Values." *Critical Studies in Television* 8, no. 2 (2013): 20–35.

Orwell, George. *The Road to Wigan Pier*. London: Mariner, 1972.

"Padma Lakshmi in Steamy New Ad for the Hardee's Western Bacon Thickburger." YouTube, April 16, 2009. Accessed June 15, 2012. https://www.youtube.com/watch?v=wNaB35-1x9M.

Padoongpatt, Mark. *Flavors of Empire: Food and the Making of Thai America*. Berkeley: University of California Press, 2017.

Palumbo-Liu, David. *Asian/American: Historical Crossings of a Racial Frontier*. Stanford, CA: Stanford University Press, 1999.

Park, Josephine Nock-Hee. *Cold War Friendships: Korea, Vietnam, and Asian American Literature*. Oxford: Oxford University Press, 2016.

Pathak, Gauri. "Delivering the Nation: The Dabbawalas of Mumbai." *South Asia: Journal of South Asian Studies* 33, no. 2 (2010): 235–57.

Patkar, Eesha. "In Conversation with: Valay Shende." *State of the Art: The Saffronart Blog* (blog), June 1, 2017. Accessed September 5, 2019. https://blog.saffronart.com /2017/06/01/in-conversation-with-valay-shende/.

Pham, Mary Jo. "Food as Communication: A Case Study of South Korea's Gastrodiplomacy." *Journal of International Service* 22, no. 1 (2013): 1–22.

Pham, Minh-Ha. "Blog Ambition: Fashion, Feelings, and the Political Economy of the Digital Raced Body." *Camera Obscura* 26, no. 1 (2015): 1–35.

Pohlhaus, Gaile, Jr. "Relational Knowing and Epistemic Injustice: Toward a Theory of *Willful Hermeneutical Ignorance*." *Hypatia* 26, no. 4 (2012): 715–35.

Potter, Lucy, and Claire Westall. "Neoliberal Britain's Austerity Foodscape: Home Economics, Veg Patch Capitalism and Culinary Temporality." *new formations* 80–81 (2013): 155–78.

Powell, Julie. *Julie & Julia*. New York: Little, Brown, 2005.

Power, Nani. *Ginger and Ganesh: Adventures in Indian Cooking, Culture and Love*. Berkeley, CA: Counterpoint, 2010.

Prashad, Vijay. *The Karma of Brown Folk*. Minneapolis: University of Minnesota Press, 2001.

Rahman, Muzna. "Covert Communications: Food in Transition in Ritesh Batra's *The Lunchbox*." *Journal of Postcolonial Writing* 54, no. 4 (2018): 484–97.

Rakowitz, Michael. *Backstroke of the West*. Chicago: Museum of Contemporary Arts Chicago and Delmonico Books, 2017.

Rana, Junaid. *Terrifying Muslims: Race and Labor in the South Asian Diaspora*. Durham, NC: Duke University Press, 2011.

Ray, Krishnendu. *The Migrant's Table: Meals and Memories in Bengali-American Households*. Philadelphia: Temple University Press, 2004.

Rich, Katherine Russell. *Dreaming in Hindi: Coming Awake in Another Language*. New York: Mariner Books, 2010. Kindle.

Rockwell, David. "Creating Public Intimacy: Designing Restaurant Booths and Banquettes." *The Atlantic*, November 8, 2011. Accessed June 15, 2020. https://www .theatlantic.com/national/archive/2011/11/creating-public-intimacy-designing -restaurant-booths-and-banquettes/248041/.

Roma, Sarina, Padma Lakshmi, and David Shadrack Smith, creators. *Taste the Nation with Padma Lakshmi*. Part 2 pictures, 2020. Hulu. https://www.hulu.com/series /taste-the-nation-with-padma-lakshmi-53d48a66-d254-4e4f-89a1-277ec6c57368.

Rosenbloom, Stephanie. *Alone Time: Four Seasons, Four Cities, and the Pleasures of Solitude*. New York: Viking, 2018.

Rubin, Gretchen. *The Happiness Project*. New York: HarperCollins, 2007.

Rushdie, Salman. *The Satanic Verses*. New York: Random House, 2008. Kindle.

Said, Edward. *Culture and Imperialism*. New York: Viking, 1994.

Sammells, Clare A., and Edmund Searles. "Restaurants, Fields, Markets, and Feasts:

Food and Culture in Semi-Public Spaces" *Food and Foodways* 24, nos. 3–4 (2016): 129–35.

Schmidt Camacho, Alicia. *Migrant Imaginaries: Latino Cultural Politics in the U.S.-Mexico Borderlands*. New York: New York University Press, 2008.

Schwartz, Alyssa. "Table for One: The Singular Joy of Dining Alone." Oprah.com. Accessed September 25, 2020. http://www.oprah.com/omagazine/how-to-dine -alone-eating-alone-at-a-restaurant.

Seen, Aveek, and Susanne Gaensheimer, eds. *Subodh Gupta: Everything Is Inside*. New Delhi: Penguin Books India, 2014.

Shah, Riddhi. "Culinary Diplomacy at the Axis of Evil Cafe." Salon.com, June 9, 2010. Accessed September 25, 2020. http://www.salon.com/2010/06/09/conflict _kitchen_restaurant/.

Shamsie, Kamila. *Home Fire*. New York: Riverhead Books, 2017. Kindle.

Shohat, Ella. "Culinary Ghosting: A Journey through a Sweet and Sour Iraq." *Crítica Cultural* 12, no. 2 (2017): 219–26.

Siu, Lok. "Twenty-First-Century Food Trucks: Mobility, Social Media, and Urban Hipness." In *Eating Asian America: A Food Studies Reader*, edited by Robert Ji-Song Ku, Martin F. Manalansan IV, and Anita Mannur, 231–44. New York: New York University Press, 2013.

Slawson, Nicola. "Jo Cox Murder Accused Gives Name as 'Death to Traitors, Freedom for Britain," *The Guardian*, June 18, 2016. Accessed June 15, 2020. https://www .theguardian.com/uk-news/2016/jun/18/jo-cox-murder-suspect-thomas-mair-told -police-he-was-political-activist.

Sohmer, Slade. "Conflict Kitchen: Its Ethnic Foods Seduce, Its Wrappers Engage." Accessed September 10, 2013. http://hypervocal.com/news/2013/conflict-kitchen/. Site no longer available.

Spiegel, Lynn. *Welcome to the Dreamhouse: Popular Media and Postwar Suburbs*. Durham, NC: Duke University Press, 2001.

Stacey, Jackie. "The Global Within: Consuming Nature, Embodying Health." In *Global Nature, Global Culture*, edited by Sarah Franklin, Celia Lury, and Jackie Stacey, 97–146. London: SAGE, 2007.

Street, Brian. *Social Literacies: Critical Approaches to Literacy in Development, Ethnography and Education*. New York: Pearson Longman, 1995.

"Subodh Gupta: Everything Is Inside at MMK Frankfurt." Designboom. Accessed September 25, 2020. http://www.designboom.com/art/subodh-gupta-everything -is-inside-mmk-frankfurt-09-11-2014/.

Tankard, Scott, dir. *The Great British Bake-Off*. Season 3, episode 10, "The Final." Aired October 16, 2012, on BBC. https://www.netflix.com/watch/80165135?trackId =200257859.

Ternikar, Farha. "Feeding the Muslim South Asian Immigrant Family: A Feminist Analysis of Culinary Consumption." In *Feminist Food Studies: Intersectional Perspectives*, edited by Barbara Parker, Jennifer Brady, Elaine M. Power, and Susan Belyea, 145–62. Toronto: Women's Press, 2019.

Tongson, Karen. *Relocations: Queer Suburban Imaginaries*. New York: New York University Press, 2011.

Trivedi-Grenier, Leena. "New Online Survey Investigates U.S. Food Blog Usage." *Leena Eats* (blog), October 6, 2011. http://www.leenaeats.com/blog/media/blogs/all/Leena eats.com_US_Food_Blog_Survey_PR_06.20.2008.pdf. Site no longer available.

Truong, Monique. *The Book of Salt*. New York: Mariner Books, 2004.

Varagur, Krithika. "The Great Brexit Bake Off." *New Yorker*, February 5, 2019. Accessed March 1, 2019. https://www.newyorker.com/humor/daily-shouts/the-great-brexit -bake-off.

Wang, Oliver. "Learning from Los Kogi Angeles: A Taco Truck and Its City." In *Eating Asian America: A Food Studies Reader*, edited by Robert Ji-Song Ku, Martin F. Manalansan IV, and Anita Mannur, 78–97. New York: New York University Press, 2013.

Warner, Michael. *Publics and Counterpublics*. New York: Zone Books, 2005.

Weinberg, Sarah. "Baking Is the Best Way to Alleviate Stress—Yes, Really." *Delish*, March 25, 2020. Accessed March 27, 2020. https://www.delish.com/food/a31669795 /stress-baking/.

Williams, Ruth. *Eat, Pray, Love*: Producing the Female Neoliberal Spiritual Subject." *Journal of Popular Culture* 47, no. 3 (2013): 613–33.

Wong, Sau-Ling. *Reading Asian American Literature: From Necessity to Extravagance*. Princeton, NJ: Princeton University Press, 1993.

Woodcock, Nicolyn. "Narratives of Intimacy in Asian American Literature." In *Encyclopedia of Asian American and Pacific Island Literatures and Culture*, edited by Josephine Lee, 1046–61. Oxford: Oxford University Press, 2000.

Xu, Wenying. *Eating Identities: Reading Food in Asian American Literature*. Honolulu: University of Hawai'i Press, 2007.

Zimmerman, Edith. "Women Laughing Alone with Salad." *The Hairpin*, January 3, 2011. Accessed January 14, 2019. https://www.thehairpin.com/2011/01/women-laughing -alone-with-salad/.

Index

Page numbers followed by *f* refer to figures.

Cox, Jo, 67, 150nn36–37
Craigslist, 18, 76, 85–89, 93, 153n37
Craigslist Killer, 87. *See also* Markoff, Philip
Crawford, Clementine, 54–55
critical ethnic studies, 15
Crouch, Tracey, 67
Cuba, 120
Cuban Americans, 122
Cuban people, 122
cultural capital, 17, 27, 80, 82–83, 103, 105, 125–26
cultural logics, 6, 18–19
cultural studies, 1
Curry Up Now, 101

dabbas/tiffins, 16–17, 23–26, 29, 31–34, 148n7, 148n12; in *The Lunchbox*, 36–37, 39–40, 44*f*
dabbawallas, 16–17, 23–31, 32*f*, 34–42, 45, 148n1, 148n13, 149n13
Dai, Lawrence: *Lawrence/Julie and Julia Project, The*, 94–96, 154n54
Derrida, Jacques, 35, 109
DESBY, 86, 89, 92
Desis, 86
Detloff, Madelyn, 65
diaspora, 57, 110; queer, 52; South Asian, 7, 11, 51, 86; Sri Lankan, 17–18, 50. *See also* Australia; Malaysia; Papua New Guinea
diaspora studies, 6
digital media, 18–19, 76–77, 86
digital racial formation, 74, 96
dining, 6, 16, 119; mobile, 101, 105, 125; public, 25, 28; solo, 14–15, 17, 51, 53–55, 59–67, 71, 143, 150n12; table, 11–12, 57, 127
Diplomatic Culinary Partnership (DCP), 126–27
domestication, 21, 86, 132
domesticity, 41–42, 64, 76–77, 94, 153n48; and *The Great British Bake Off*, 139–40; and shared meals, 12, 14
domestic spaces, 6, 57, 62; and dabbawallas, 16, 24, 29, 30, 36, 51
domestic work, 30, 37, 64

Easy Slider, 101
Eat Pray Love (2010 film, dir. Ryan Murphy), 6, 18, 53, 90–91. *See also* Gilbert, Elizabeth

Eat St., 100
Elam, Michele, 3
embodiment, 4, 10, 16, 64–65, 101, 125, 127
enemy, concept of, 8, 19–20, 125, 127; and food, 106–20
Enemy Kitchen, 7, 19–20, 106–22, 125, 127
Eng, David L., 96
England, 104, 133–38, 158n16; London, 129. *See also* Brexit; Great Britain; United Kingdom
Ephron, Nora, 74. See also *Julie & Julia* (film)
epistemology, 61, 124–27
epistles, 36, 40. *See also* letters
epistolarity, 17, 23–24, 35, 37, 149n31. *See also* letters; *Lunchbox, The*
Erickson, Karla, 6
ethnic studies, 1, 15, 50
ethnoburbs, 89
ethnography, 34, 50, 81, 85, 88, 103
Europe, 3, 104, 137. *See also* England; France; Germany; Great Britain; Italy; United Kingdom
European Community, 138, 158n9
European cuisine, 136
European Union Referendum Campaign, 150n36. *See also* Brexit

Facebook, 74, 99–100, 120
failure, concept of, 27, 36; in *The Lunchbox*, 35–46; queer, 18, 49, 65–71
family, 5, 36, 146; chosen, 14, 143; heteronormative, 16, 50–51, 63; nuclear, 10–12, 14, 36–37, 51, 61, 145; South Asian, 17, 36, 61, 66. *See also* kinship
femininity, 77, 82, 84
feminism, 30, 50, 54, 94, 146; white middle-class, 18–19, 74, 77
Florida: Miami, 99
Fluxus movement, 105, 110, 154n11
food carts, 100, 124–25, 127, 155n21. *See also* food trucks; loncheras
food delivery, 17, 145; and dabbawallas, 24–25, 29–31, 34, 39–40, 149n13
food delivery apps, 25. *See also* Grubhub; Swiggy; Uber Eats; Zomato
Food Network, 89, 100
food pornography, 60, 83. *See also* gastro-pornography

food studies, 6, 9–10, 14, 30, 50

food trucks, 4, 19, 99–105, 117, 120, 151n6, 154n3, 155n34; and *Enemy Kitchen*, 111–15, 122, 124–25, 127. See also *Enemy Kitchen;* food carts; loncheras

food vending, 24, 124–26, 156n47

foodways, 8, 50–51, 66, 81, 85

food writers, 31, 54, 75–76, 100, 102

Forbes, 28, 34–35

foreignness, 4, 21, 77, 103, 106, 147n9

France, 83, 94, 96; Paris, 73, 80, 82, 84, 152n27, 154n54

Freedman, Josh, 139

French colonialism, 94

French cuisine, 73, 77–84, 94–95, 152nn26–27, 154n54

gastro-pornography, 63. *See also* food pornography

gender, 5, 50–51, 57, 110, 131, 157n50; and dabbawallas, 24, 29–34; and the internet, 19, 77, 93; in *The Lunchbox*, 41–42. *See also* femininity; patriarchy

gender studies, 50

Germany: Frankfurt, 27

Gilbert, Elizabeth: *Eat, Pray, Love* (book), 6, 18, 53, 90–91

globalization, 18, 28, 89–91, 105, 147n9

Global South, 43

Glowfish, 102

Gold, Jonathan, 102

"good life," 7–9, 11, 46, 51, 139–40

Gopinath, Gayatri, 7, 52, 126

Great Britain, 20–21, 61, 67, 129–32, 134–39, 150n36. *See also* Brexit; British colonialism; Britishness; England; United Kingdom

Great British Bake Off, The (GBBO), 6, 20–21, 134–45, 157n2, 157n7, 158n10, 158n12; and Britishness, 130–32

Great British Baking Show, The. See Great British Bake Off, The (GBBO)

Great Food Truck Race, The, 100

Grill Em All, 102

Grubhub, 25

Guac n'Roll, 101

Gupta, Subodh, 27, 148n7

Hage, Ghassan, 77

Halberstam, Jack, 18, 36, 66–67

Hall, Radclyffe, 52

Hall, Stuart, 136

Hardee's, 60

Harris, Gardiner, 23, 148n1

Haudenosaunee Confederacy, 120, 123

Heathrow Airport, 129

hegemony of vision, 1

Heidegger, Martin, 78–80, 92

Hernandez, Michael, 20

Hernandez-Lopez, Ernesto, 103

heteronormativity, 5, 16, 18, 46, 62, 79; and the family, 11–12, 14, 63–64; and food, 50–51, 66; and the good life, 7–8; and marriage, 30, 37, 41, 61

heterosexuality, 13, 61, 66, 133

heterotopia, 61, 88

heuristics, 9–10

Highmore, Ben, 93

Holden, Stephen, 99

Hollywood, Paul, 132, 145, 157n8

homophobia, 6, 13, 65

hooks, bell, 77

Hopper, Edward, 68

hospitality, 19; radical, 20, 106, 119, 124, 127

Hussain, Nadiya, 21, 132–35

Hussein, Saddam, 117–18, 118f

Illinois: Chicago, 68, 106, 111–12, 112f, 119

immigrant food, 13, 75, 85, 148n20

immigrants, 3, 10, 31, 61, 88, 92, 106, 157n9; Afghan, 107; Asian, 81–82; and *The Great British Bake Off*, 133, 135, 138; Indian, 76, 89; Iraqi, 115, 117; Muslim, 131; in New York City, 80–82, 156n47; Pakistani, 124–25; racialized, 60, 147n16; South Asian, 134; Southeast Asian, 95; Vietnamese, 95. *See also* Afghan Americans; Asian Americans; Desis; Indian Americans; Iraqi Americans; Mexican Americans; Pakistani Americans; Pakistani British people; refugees; South Asians

imperialism, 1, 6, 18; Anglo-American, 83; British, 136–37, 138; US, 9, 107, 109, 117, 152n23. *See also* British colonialism; colonialism; French colonialism; Said, Edward

India, 3, 17, 25, 28, 83, 91, 148n7; Bangalore, 53;

Lower Manhattan Development Corporation (LMDC), 78–79
Lucas, Matt, 145
Lunchbox, The, 6, 17, 23–26, 49, 149n31; and failure, 35–46

Mair, Thomas, 67–68, 150n36
Makan, Chetna, 134
Malaysia, 11
Maliki, Nouri al-, 119
Manalansan, Martin, IV, 64, 81, 85
Mandal, Rahul, 132–34, 136
Mani, Bakirathi, 57
Mannur, Anita: Culinary Fictions, 9
Marathi language, 29, 36, 148n11
Markoff, Philip, 87
Marx, Karl, 139
Massachusetts: Amherst, 13; Salem, 26
May, Theresa, 67
McFate, Robert: After Hopper, 69–70, 70f
Mead, Rebecca, 68
Medge, Raghunath, 30–31, 34–35
Mediterranean cuisine, 114
Mehta, Mithila, 28
methodology of the book, 4–10, 15–21
Mexican Americans, 101
Mexican cuisine, 103–4. See also Korean Mexican fusion cuisine
Mexicans, 100
Michelin Guides, 15
microblogging, 75, 125–26, 151n6. See also Twitter
middle class, 24, 29–30, 40, 104, 148n7; white feminists, 19, 74, 77, 82–84; white women, 18, 90–92
Middle Eastern cuisine, 8, 108, 110, 114
migration, 17–18, 89, 114
Mill, John Stuart, 158n16
Mills, Charles, 87
Minister of Loneliness, 67
Modern Language Association (MLA), 102
Mohanraj, Mary Anne: Bodies in Motion, 6, 17, 50, 55, 61, 64, 66
Mountbatten, Louis, 83
multiculturalism, 21, 66, 88, 106, 109, 152n26; and food trucks, 101, 104, 114, 117, 120, 126–27; and The Great British Bake Off, 132,

134–35, 137–38, 157n7; neoliberal, 5–6, 10–11, 19, 51, 77, 90–94
Mumbai Tiffinmen's Association, 34
Museum für Moderne Kunst (Frankfurt), 27
Muslim Americans, 107–8
Muslims, 107, 125, 129; Shias, 130; Sunnis, 130. See also Islam

Nacho Bizness, 101
Naficy, Hamid, 35
Nakamura, Lisa, 74, 76
National Association of Negro Women conference, 84
National Health Service, 145
nationalism, 15–16, 65, 133, 153n36
Nazis, 47
Nello (restaurant), 54
neoliberalism, 101, 104; and multiculturalism, 5–6, 10–11, 19, 51, 77, 90–94
Nepalese cuisine, 13
New England, 74
New Formations, 93
New Jersey, 80, 89
New York City, 17, 93, 117–18, 118f, 124–25, 134, 151n6, 156n47; Brooklyn, 114; East Village, 58f, 107; Manhattan, 54; Queens, 77–85, 91–92, 95–96, 152n27
New Yorker, 68, 137
New York Times, 23, 54, 99, 151n7
Ngai, Sianne, 111
Nguyen, Mimi Thi, 117
Nom Nom, 102
nonnormativity, 4–6, 9–11, 88, 143
normativity, 7–8, 10–11, 16, 24, 49–56, 60, 65, 71; and The Lunchbox, 43, 45
North Korea, 120, 123–24, 155n35
"North Korean Cooking Lesson," 123
North Korean cuisine, 123
Northwestern University, 94
Nutan Tiffin Box Suppliers Charity Trust, 31

Obama, Barack, 119, 126–27
Obama, Michelle, 126, 156n50
Office of Strategic Services (US), 82, 152n23
Ohio, 75; Cincinnati, 13, 69; Columbus, 74; Oxford, 13

US immigration policy, 89
US State Department, 119, 126–27
US Transportation Security Administration, 130
Uzbek cuisine, 13

Varagur, Krithika, 137–38
Venezuela, 120
Venezuelan cuisine, 123
Vietnamese cuisine, 94–96
Vietnamese people, 154n54
Vietnam Veterans against the War, 115
Virginia, 76, 85, 90, 92

Warner, Michael, 4–5
Washington, DC, 77, 84, 88
Webex, 124
Weleski, Dawn, 120, 123
Westall, Claire, 138, 140
West Indies, 158n16
White House, 126–27
whiteness, 80, 82, 84–85, 88, 96, 133, 154n54; and food, 76–77, 90–94; and middle class women, 18, 56, 73–74; privilege of, 19, 30, 83
white supremacy, 6, 67, 108, 153n36
Whitman College, 1

willfulness, 77, 82, 85–87, 94, 107, 110, 140
Williams, Ruth, 90
Wisconsin: Madison, 12–13
women, 11–12, 23, 65, 89, 131, 133, 153n48; of color, 19, 59, 75–77, 86–88, 93, 129; eating alone, 14, 54, 56–57, 60, 150n12; invisible labor of, 30, 40–42, 50–52, 63–64; single, 17–18, 55, 61; white, 18, 73, 90–92, 96. *See also* DESBY
Woodcock, Nicolyn, 9
Woolf, Virginia, 15
working class, 40, 100–101, 103–4, 124
World Trade Center, 79
World Trade Organization, 137
World War II, 73–74

xenophobia, 4, 65, 108, 115, 133, 135, 139, 158n9; cultural, 20, 107. *See also* Brexit

Yelp, 95
Yun, Zheng, 57

Zimmerman, Edith, 56
Zomato, 25
Zoom, 124